GET UNSTUCK
AND
MOVE FORWARD WITH YOUR LIFE

GET UNSTUCK *and Move Forward With Your Life*
Unlock Your Potential and Create the Life You Deserve

Jason Hopcus

©2024 All Rights Reserved. No portion of this book may be reproduced, stored in a retrieval system, or transmitted in any form or by any means-electronic, mechanical, photocopy, recording, scanning, or other-except for brief quotations in critical reviews or articles without the prior permission of the author.

Published by Game Changer Publishing

Paperback ISBN: 978-1-964811-87-1
Hardcover ISBN: 978-1-964811-85-7
Digital ISBN: 978-1-964811-86-4

www.GameChangerPublishing.com

Dedication

To everyone who shaped my story:
My family, whose lessons and support propelled me forward,
My dear friend Garnette, whose unwavering support breathed life into these words, and my love, Gus, whose commitment and belief in me marked the true beginning of my life. This book is a testament to the countless stories and experiences that have molded me and to every person who has contributed along the way.
With wholehearted gratitude.

–Jason

Read This First

To say thank you for buying and reading my book,
I would like to give you a couple of free bonus gifts

Download Your Free Gifts

My Honesty Report Card and the Plutchik Emotion Wheel
to guide you through your journey.
No strings attached - enjoy!

Scan the QR Code:

GET UNSTUCK

and

Move Forward With Your Life

Unlock Your Potential and
Create the Life You Deserve

Jason Hopcus

www.GameChangerPublishing.com

Table of Contents

Author's Note 1

Introduction: Embracing Transformation to Create a New Mindset 3

Part I: Facing the Past to Forge Ahead 9
    Houses With Weak Foundations Cannot Stand 11
    Finding Strength From Community 15
    Courage Over Comfort 20
    Everyone Struggles 24
    Is the Hard Work Worth it? 29
    Unraveled 33
    Wherever You Go, There You Are 39
    Seeing Your Reflection 43
    Confronting Childhood Shadows 45

Part II: Turning Setbacks Into Strength 49
    Value of Being Vulnerable 51
    Facing Our Fears Head-on 55
    Vulnerability Leads to Authenticity 59
    Breakdowns Lead to Breakthroughs 62
    Checking Your Inner Critic 75
    Owning Your Role 81
    Failure to Move You Forward 87
    Using Pain In Purpose 98

Part III: Taking Steps to Support Yourself 103
    Progressing to Growth and Fulfillment 105
    Claiming Your Worth With Self-Care 110
    Dialing in Your Vision 118
    Discovering Your Boundaries 123

    Setting Healthy Boundaries 134
    Supporting Yourself with Consistency and Care 138

Part IV: Living Empowered and Unstuck **143**
    Making Gratitude a Daily Practice 145
    Living in the Present Moment 149
    Overcoming Isolation 154
    Connecting Among Community 162
    Choosing Happiness 169
    The Unstoppable Power of Hope 173

Conclusion: Living Unstuck 177

Author's Note

First, my name is Jason Hopcus, and I am not an expert. And I am not here to "fix" you or give an expert or licensed opinion about your circumstances. What I am is someone with living experience. Someone who has endured tough times and knows the profound pain of loss and disconnection but made it to the other side. My only goal is this—to share my experience and to walk alongside you as we navigate life's challenges together. Through our journey, we will explore the gifts that come from forging a deep connection with ourselves, which then extends to meaningful connections with others.

This book is a guide, not from a place of authority but from a place of collective experience. I understand the struggles you may be facing because I have faced them, too. I know what it feels like to be stuck, to feel alone, and to yearn for something more. My hope is that through my stories and the stories of those who have helped me, the insights you find in the following pages will give you the strength and courage to uncover your own path of healing and growth.

We will dig deep into the power of vulnerability, the importance of self-compassion, and the transformative impact of genuine human connection. You will discover that your struggles don't define your worthiness. Instead, they are the fertile ground from which your true purpose can emerge. By facing our difficulties without fear, we can gain a deeper understanding of ourselves and the world around us.

In sharing our truths, we discover we are not alone. We find solace in knowing that others have walked similar paths and have found their way through. This connection allows everything else to start falling into place.

I invite you to join me on this journey. Together, we will navigate life's challenges, embrace vulnerability, and uncover the gifts within ourselves. Let's walk this path side by side, discovering the profound connections that will transform our lives.

Are you ready to take the next step?

Introduction
Embracing Transformation
to Create a New Mindset

In chasing my dream life, I once believed material success would heal the wounds of my past. Despite achieving significant monetary success, I struggled with a lifetime of emotional scars and an overwhelming sense of inadequacy. My relentless pursuit of validation through materialism crumbled when I realized the truth: Genuine self-acceptance is the key to inner healing, far beyond any external accolade.

Get Unstuck and Move Forward With Your Life is dedicated to and written for those who have faced setbacks yet recognize their current path falls short of their truest aspirations. It speaks directly to the heart of individuals who have tried various methods to break free from stagnation, only to find themselves still struggling with familiar challenges.

This book supports:

- People who have enough self-awareness to know that while this book offers guidance, it is not a replacement for professional support during times of significant distress.
- Those who reject harsh methods and unrealistic promises and understand that transformation requires compassion and sustainable effort.

- Individuals possessing a keen sense of discernment regarding the excuses we all use to avoid taking meaningful action.
- Readers who have tried other self-help methods before and are looking for a deeper, more nuanced approach.
- Anyone who acknowledges that putting others' needs ahead of their own is often an excuse rather than a genuine barrier to personal growth.
- Those who recognize their challenges may stem from complex sources beyond surface-level issues.
- People who have experienced or rejected the intensity of boot camp-style life transformations and seek a more balanced, sustainable path.
- Those wary of books promising miraculous solutions and comprehend that real progress requires ongoing commitment and revisitation.
- Individuals who are willing to confront the hard work of addressing past traumas as a crucial step towards personal evolution and success.

Get Unstuck and Move Forward With Your Life does not promise a quick fix or claim to be the ultimate solution to the challenges we all can face. Instead, it offers a compassionate roadmap for those ready to embark on a journey of self-discovery and growth. It's an invitation to let go of excuses, embrace self-compassion, and take decisive steps towards a brighter future. You are more than your story.

Embracing Transformation

This is your call to reclaim your narrative, understand your history, and recognize that you can define your destiny.

Your experiences, even the most painful ones, can become a source of strength and inspiration for others. Your journey through adversity provides you with the empathy, passion, and wisdom needed to discover and fulfill your purpose. One day, you'll look back on your challenges with gratitude, recognizing how each obstacle shaped you into the person you aspire to be. Embracing and sharing your unique story will not only empower you but also encourage others on their own paths.

As you move forward, keep your focus on the horizon of hope while remaining true to your values. Treat yourself with compassion and love, knowing your worth and the potential within you.

> *You are not defined by your past, constrained by circumstances, or irreparably broken. You are resilient, capable, and prepared for the journey ahead.*

Welcome this transformation with open arms, for the power to change resides within you. If you're yearning for deeper fulfillment and sense that a more rewarding life awaits, consider this book your companion on the path to liberation. The journey toward personal empowerment begins with a single courageous step—the step towards the life you truly deserve.

Creating a New Mindset

As you embark on this transformative journey, we will walk a path of self-discovery and growth grounded in the following principles:

- **Illusions and Expectations.** We will reflect on the illusions and expectations that have shaped your pursuit of success and happiness.

Together, we will find a balance between external achievements and inner fulfillment, helping you redefine what true success means for you.

- **Authenticity and Healing.** You will be encouraged to explore your truest authenticity and confront your past. By doing so, you will experience positive transformations, ensuring that your pursuit of external achievements never comes at the expense of your inner well-being.

- **Resilience and Growth.** Navigating challenges without a clear roadmap can be daunting, but you will learn to recognize that hardships do not define your worthiness. Instead, they prepare you for growth and resilience, shaping you into a stronger, more capable individual.

- **Actions Lead to Awakenings.** Intentional actions will propel you forward. You will embrace failure as an opportunity to learn and grow, redefining your struggles as stepping stones toward a clearer purpose. Each step you take will bring you closer to your truest potential.

- **Living Beyond the Illusion.** You will discover a profound sense of worthiness, learn to set boundaries, practice gratitude, and choose happiness as a daily commitment. Hope will become your steadfast companion, guiding you through life's challenges with unwavering faith.

- **Gratitude and Happiness.** Cultivating gratitude will help you find silver linings in life's challenges. You will learn to choose happiness as a daily practice rooted in mindfulness and intentional perspective shifts that enrich your life.

- **Taking Small Steps.** We will overcome resistance to taking small steps together. You will commit to consistency, understanding that lasting positive change is achieved through small, consistent actions aligned with your values.

- **Ownership and Empowerment.** You will take ownership of your path, surround yourself with positive support, and consistently take the next right step. True progress is slow and non-linear, but you will embrace this journey with patience and determination.
- **Compassion and Self-Acceptance.** Judgment will be replaced with compassion for yourself. You will reframe self-critical thoughts and find meaning in negative experiences, nurturing a mindset of abundance and self-love.
- **Hope and Courage.** Hope will be your guiding force. You will nurture it and let it guide you forward, understanding that the life you desire is not just a distant vision but a promise fueled by the enduring flame of hope.

Get Unstuck and Move Forward With Your Life will become your trusted companion toward a more fulfilling life. Together, we will navigate the complexities of existence, turning challenges into opportunities for growth and discovering the profound potential within you.

Lean into this adventure with an open heart and mind, and I promise you will find the strength, resilience, and inspiration to create the life you've always dreamed of.

PART I

Facing the Past to Forge Ahead

Houses With Weak Foundations Cannot Stand

Having experienced significant wealth and success early in my 20s, my passage from riches to rags serves as a reminder of how empty prosperity can feel after one sacrifices one's soul in the relentless chase for external validation. As my carefully constructed world fell apart, it revealed a crucial lesson that true fulfillment comes from within and the importance of self-improvement in achieving genuine happiness.

But that isn't where my story started.

From an early age, I embraced the captivating notion that grit, ingenuity, and intelligence could open the doors to limitless prosperity. My beliefs took shape under the influence of a smart, unmistakably Southern mother who was overly concerned with appearances, an emotionally unavailable father, and a verbally abusive, alcoholic stepfather.

Under the care of my mother and stepfather, I was surrounded by the prosperity of their successful construction business. However, our family prioritized business above all else, including me. As an only child (until I was ten), I was essentially a latchkey kid who tended to many of my own daily needs. In contrast, my much younger siblings had their needs met by a nanny.

Beneath the facade of apparent prosperity lay a complex tapestry of intermittent happiness and persistent heartache. My childhood was marked by emotional and sexual abuse, addiction, bullying, and divorced and emotionally absent parents who were deeply enmeshed in new marriages with spouses who effectively put their own needs first.

Each circumstance contributed to an unpredictable home life that kept me walking on eggshells and hypervigilant to the moods of everyone around me.

To outsiders, our life appeared as that of an upper-middle-class family striving for the hallmarks of success. However, behind the curtain was a boy starved for attention and yearning for love from those incapable of providing it.

From a young age, I retreated into a rich interior life. One where I clung to a vision that having enough zeros in my bank account would allow me the kind of opportunities I had only seen in movies. A world that enabled me to bypass gatekeepers and enter a realm of privilege far beyond what I had already experienced.

I would sketch floor plans for my future mansion, obsessing over every minute detail. It was the '80s, and TV series like *Dynasty* and *Dallas* were aspirational roadmaps that I was sure would lead to my imagined future as a successful attorney, complete with a Rolls Royce in my garage.

Nurturing the Illusion

As adulthood beckoned, my carefully constructed ideal became the scaffolding for my future success. With relentless determination, I wove together a new illusion: a world where I wielded control over a flawless life, a facade of empowerment to mask my true, vulnerable self.

The longer I hid behind this fabrication, the more I felt the emptiness beginning to build. I yearned for genuine connection, to be seen and understood. In the absence of true connection, I steadfastly clung to the character I played. My fragility and fear were concealed behind this character's false confidence.

After college, I joined the family construction business. It turned out to be an experience marked by considerable emotional pain. My earliest days were spent in an office, sandwiched between my mom and stepfather, while they vented their frustrations toward each other in unhealthy ways.

Eventually, I carved my own niche in real estate investing, with my mom backing my first property flip. Her lifetime of hard work and financial support inspired me to pursue my own dreams, believing they would lead to my eventual success. This initial step laid the foundation for a thriving career. Yet, despite my success, I struggled to envision a life beyond relentless hard work, always hoping it would eventually become what I'd always imagined.

Driven by the pursuit of the "dream life," I dove headfirst into building a luxury real estate empire to rival the most glamorous flippers on TV. Like many others before me, though, I came to a profound realization: When the inside is neglected and incomplete, even the most beautiful exteriors won't shine.

In the aftermath of the 2008 financial crisis, my carefully curated life crumbled. Savvy investments became financial albatrosses, stretching me and my businesses to the breaking point.

A profound sense of failure overcame me as my external validations evaporated. The beautiful houses, exotic cars, and general affluence all revealed themselves to be an elusive success that was never truly mine. The market exposed the hollow aspect of "living the dream" that society elevated—an illusion I had structured my entire identity around.

My facade of success, meticulously maintained to avoid scrutiny, served as both my armor and my prison—a paradoxical refuge shielding me from judgment but stifling my authenticity.

Staying busy kept the demons at bay for a while until life really shook things up. Clarity and impact started with the gradual unmasking of a facade. For me, it was a painful breakup, the loss of my professional identity, and financial ruin that shattered my world. In just a few short years, I went from the peak of success to almost homeless and completely aimless. I found myself drowning in debt and experiencing the darkest depression I had ever known—isolated and utterly exhausted.

My mom and dad pleaded with me to seek help, but the concept alone seemed unreachable. Enveloped in a lifetime of pain and relying on old coping skills that had barely sustained my existence up to that point, I felt lost and unsure of where to begin.

I was out of options: *emotionally, financially,* and *spiritually.*

Begrudgingly, yet no longer self-sufficient, I agreed to move in with my dad and stepmother. I spent the next few months white-knuckling each day, too proud and ashamed to ask anyone for help. I relied on my dad's steady counsel to guide me toward the next right step. Anything more was too hard to admit to anyone, let alone myself. I was drowning. Aside from my parents, there was no lifeline in sight; I believed I'd burned too many bridges in my undoing. I was unwilling to connect.

I barely left the house, didn't shave or cut my hair, lost a considerable amount of weight, and was checked out on virtually every level.

I had hit rock bottom.

After months of isolation, I finally gathered the energy to leave the house. On Halloween Eve, I ventured to a nearby Walmart and wandered aimlessly through the store. In the hunting and camping section, my crippling depression left me searching for a way to end my life, as suicide seemed like the only option to stop my unrelenting pain. Overwhelmed, I walked out of the store. As I made my way through, I passed party-ready costumed shoppers, people picking out candy for trick-or-treaters, and parents with children shopping for last-minute costumes. Seeing Little Red Riding Hood and Batman outfits made me realize the costumes of my old life were gone. I had no idea what to do next.

And then it got worse. A lot worse!

Finding Strength From Community

Life is like a long highway winding with both exhilarating highs and daunting lows. As we navigate it, seeking support can make all the difference in how we handle its challenges. It's important to understand that healing requires a range of support beyond what we can provide for ourselves. This is completely normal.

My own healing has involved experts who provided essential guidance to keep me moving forward. It has also come from the unlikely connection of those I never expected. The most mundane interaction at a bagel shop, a neighbor twice my age, or a friendship I thought irreparable. At times, it was simply surviving from week to week to eventually dig deep enough to unearth a lifetime of complex trauma.

Taking the brave step to read this book acknowledges that you've felt stuck and that you recognize your need for additional support. On this journey, you must decide whether you can do the work on your own or if you need professional help. That decision is up to you and you alone. Just know there is no shame in admitting you may require extra help to achieve your goals.

Let's explore the various ways we can leverage the strength of our communities, the expertise of professionals, and the wisdom of mentors to move forward with resilience and purpose. At best, I hope there will be parts of my story that resonate with you. At the very least, I hope you gain some practical exercises to inspire the smallest change within yourself.

The Power of Community

Our friends and family are often our first line of defense against life's difficulties. Their emotional support, diverse perspectives, and gentle reminders can help us stay on track and maintain our well-being. However, it's crucial to accept and forgive their limitations, understanding that people can only meet you from their own experience, and most people intend to do the best they know how—even when it's not what we really need. By embracing this reality, we can maintain realistic expectations and appreciate the efforts they make to support us. When we find this acceptance of others, especially family, we foster stronger, more compassionate relationships.

However, there are times when seeking professional support beyond our family and immediate circle becomes necessary to gain specialized expertise and guidance tailored to our unique challenges.

How have you utilized support that was not from family or friends?

_____

_____

_____

What other community resources do you know of that can help you connect?

_____

_____

_____

Professional Guidance

Recognizing that some struggles are more deeply rooted and require specialized support, professional guidance can offer the structured expertise needed for profound change. If you find yourself in difficult situations, here are some support options you might consider:

- **Psychotherapy and Counseling.** Trained therapists help us explore deep-rooted issues and develop coping strategies, providing emotional and psychological support tailored to our needs.
- **Life Coaches.** These professionals assist with setting and achieving personal and professional goals, helping us overcome obstacles and realize our full potential.
- **Career Counseling.** For those facing professional stagnation or seeking new career paths, career counselors offer tailored advice and strategies for navigating your career objectives.
- **Financial Counseling.** Financial challenges often underlie other obstacles. Financial counselors provide structured advice on budgeting, debt management, and financial planning.
- **Health and Wellness Coaches.** These experts guide us in adopting healthy habits, managing stress, and making sustainable lifestyle changes.
- **Specialized Therapeutic Modalities.** Techniques for addressing trauma or for emotional regulation can be crucial for addressing specific mental health challenges. These treatments must be administered by trained clinicians.
- **Psychiatric Support.** When mental health issues require medication, psychiatric professionals integrate therapy and medication for comprehensive care.
- **Legal and Financial Advisers.** Some struggles involve legal or financial complexities, and professional advice is essential for navigating these areas effectively.

- **Educational Consultants.** Whether dealing with academic struggles or career-related decisions, educational consultants help align our educational paths with our aspirations.
- **Personal Development Seminars and Workshops.** Engaging in expert-led workshops provides tools and insights for self-discovery and growth.
- **Community Resources.** Beyond professional help, free community resources offer additional support. Joining groups with shared experiences, such as twelve-step programs or support groups for specific challenges, can provide a sense of belonging and mutual encouragement.
- **Faith-based Resources and Secular Gatherings.** Tailored to our spiritual beliefs or personal histories can also be invaluable.

Integrating Your Support Network

As you take each step, community is a beacon of light guiding you toward a life unburdened by stagnation. Each member of your support network can propel you toward a brighter future. By leaning on the rich experience of your community, you will likely find the strength, resilience, and inspiration needed to forge ahead with confidence and purpose.

Together, we will examine our struggles and the ways we've allowed challenging chapters to define us and hold us back from progressing. This involves exploring the most painful parts of our past—a vital step towards releasing burdens and moving forward. Through personal stories and shared experiences, the aim is to foster connection and understanding. While each story is unique, the challenges we face are universally relatable. It is my hope you find solace and gain insight from the shared wisdom and empathy woven into practical steps toward self-healing and growth:

- **Reflect and Acknowledge.** Take time to reflect on past experiences without judgment. Acknowledge the emotions and lessons learned from challenging chapters.
- **Seek Support.** Reach out to trusted friends, family, or a therapist for emotional support and guidance. Sharing your story with empathetic listeners can be incredibly healing.
- **Practice Self-Compassion.** Treat yourself with kindness and understanding. Embrace self-compassion as a way to nurture resilience and self-acceptance during difficult times.

These steps aim to offer clarity amidst life's uncertainties, emphasizing the importance of moving forward with self-compassion and understanding.

This process will empower you to understand that your past does not dictate your future. By taking the first step, you open up abundant possibilities ahead. You have the power to get unstuck and move forward; progress awaits those who summon the courage to act.

Courage Over Comfort

Your willingness to confront what holds you back demonstrates self-awareness. It indicates your readiness to address familiar yet unproductive thinking patterns that hinder progress. We've all experienced moments like these—stuck in old mindsets, facing common obstacles that can block our growth and happiness. Recognizing this is a first step toward significant change.

Comfort in the Familiar

The old mindset is a comfort zone, a place where we revert to familiar thoughts and behaviors even when they no longer serve us. You know those times when you can't seem to get out of your own way? It's the inner voice that tells us to stay safe, to avoid risks, and to stick with what we know. This mindset can be a protective mechanism, but it limits our potential and keeps us from exploring new possibilities. By exploring this now, you've shown a desire to break free from these limiting beliefs and discover a more expansive view of your capabilities.

Common Roadblocks

The usual suspects are recurring themes and obstacles that consistently appear in our lives, hindering our progress. These obstacles can manifest in various forms:

- **Self-Doubt.** This is the inner critic that questions your abilities and worthiness, often leading to hesitation and second-guessing.
- **Fear of Failure.** This is the anxiety that paralyzes you at the thought of making mistakes or falling short of expectations, preventing you from taking necessary risks.
- **Procrastination.** This is the tendency to delay actions or decisions, which can be driven by perfectionism, fear of failure, or feeling overwhelmed by tasks.
- **Negative Self-Talk.** This is the habit of focusing on your flaws, shortcomings, or past mistakes instead of recognizing your strengths and achievements, which can diminish self-confidence.
- **Resistance to Change.** This is the reluctance to step out of your comfort zone, embrace new opportunities, or make necessary adjustments in your life, even when they could lead to personal growth.

Identifying your common roadblocks is crucial as it helps you recognize patterns that may be holding you back. By acknowledging and addressing these challenges, you can begin to overcome them and move forward toward your goals with greater clarity and determination.

What are the roadblocks that have or are currently standing in your way?

_____

_____

_____

Courage to Change

Change begins with honesty and the willingness to examine our current mindset critically. It involves asking tough questions about why we hold onto certain beliefs and behaviors. Start by asking yourself:

Are your beliefs truly serving you, or are they remnants of past fears and insecurities?

_____

_____

_____

Your decision to take a deeper look reflects a readiness to challenge these old patterns and to replace them with more empowering and constructive ones.

Framing a New Perspective

Through this transformative journey, you'll discover strategies to replace limiting mindsets with a positive, growth-oriented perspective. You'll be encouraged to:
- **Cultivate Self-Compassion.** Treat yourself with the same kindness and understanding you would offer a friend.
- **Embrace Failure as Learning.** View mistakes as opportunities to grow and learn rather than as definitive judgments of your worth.
- **Take Small, Consistent Steps.** Recognize that progress is often incremental and that small, consistent actions lead to significant changes over time.
- **Foster a Growth Mindset.** Believe in your capacity to change and improve through effort and perseverance.

- **Build a Supportive Network.** Surround yourself with people who encourage and inspire you, providing the support needed to navigate challenges.

By addressing the usual roadblocks and adopting new strategies, which we will continue to discuss, you will pave the way for a more fulfilling and resilient approach to life.

Forging the Journey Ahead

I cannot promise the journey ahead will be easy, but it will be deeply rewarding. You've already demonstrated the openness and self-awareness needed to begin this journey. *Get Unstuck and Move Forward With Your Life* will serve as your guide, offering insights and practical advice to help you more smoothly navigate the ups and downs of personal growth. Remember, the fact you've chosen to embark on this path shows your willingness for change and your commitment to creating a better, more fulfilling life.

Everyone Struggles

The realization that struggle is a shared human experience—perceived through each person's unique lens—transforms it into an opportunity for personal growth. For years, I clung to an old belief and lie from childhood that struggle equaled failure, hoping each new achievement would finally make life easier.

What I've learned in my own journey of getting unstuck is that struggle signifies stretching toward the next phase of becoming. A place within where we can live boldly from a leading edge instead of letting complacency stall us. Each difficult choice prepares us for a more intentional response the next time we need to act.

Behind the curated facade of "perfect" lives, every single one of us will face struggles. We are a society of imperfection. We have an unlimited capacity for joy but, at the same time, the ability to feel fear and let it control us. We can be both excited and scared, hopeful and worried, or ambitious and insecure—all at the same time. It is this uniqueness that makes us human.

The Lies We Tell Ourselves

The tendency to compare our lives with others is common and often driven by the desire to competitively measure progress, success, and fulfillment. Engaging in this practice creates the risk of oversimplification and misunderstanding, especially when the complexities shaping each person's journey are unknown. Social media perpetuates a distorted reality, showcasing only curated highlight reels that never actually reveal what lies behind the curtain.

I constantly compared myself to others, especially with regard to how I viewed their success versus mine. I saw friends and acquaintances achieving milestones I felt I was missing. Their professional accomplishments, happy relationships, and perfectly arranged vacations made me feel inadequate and left behind.

One particular instance stands out vividly. A close friend shared news of a significant promotion at work, complete with celebratory dinner photos and congratulatory comments from our mutual friends. I genuinely wanted to be happy for her, but it triggered a wave of self-doubt. I began questioning my own career trajectory, wondering if I was progressing too slowly or had made the wrong choices altogether. Despite my own success, it seemed insignificant at that moment compared to her achievement.

It took time and reflection to realize that I was only seeing a small, polished part of her life. I hadn't considered the late nights, the stress, or the sacrifices she made to reach that point. Was I not guilty of showcasing my success through beautiful houses, expensive artwork, luxury clothes, and rare cars? I easily dismissed my achievements compared to someone who had climbed a different mountain. This is how I compared my "insides" (i.e., my feelings) to others' "outsides" (i.e., what I showed the world).

Comparison is a Thief

Comparing myself to others based on such limited information was not only unfair but also damaging. It overshadowed my achievements and created unnecessary anxiety. I had to remind myself that everyone's path is unique and shaped by different challenges and opportunities. What's more, I have finally learned to celebrate my progress, however small it might seem in comparison, and to appreciate the individuality of my path.

Empathy is essential, both toward ourselves and others. Every individual's story is influenced by a multitude of factors; making direct comparisons is not only unproductive but also objectively inaccurate. We are each uniquely ourselves.

This shift in perspective helped me focus more on my growth and less on external validation. I began setting goals that were meaningful to me and finding fulfillment in my own accomplishments, regardless of how they stacked up against others. It was a liberating experience that allowed me to move forward with more confidence and contentment.

Through this process, I discovered the importance of self-compassion and the value of staying true to myself. By letting go of the constant comparisons, I found greater peace and a deeper sense of purpose, understanding that my worth is not determined by how I measure up to others but by how I live authentically and passionately.

Amidst societal struggles, we hesitate to reveal what we perceive as our weaknesses for fear they might erode our worth in cultures that are hyperfocused on predicting success. For years, I privately fought deep-rooted shame, but then I chose to face the past and open up. Today, I choose transparency in the hope that my story of struggle makes you feel less alone in your own.

Courage does not reside in appearing invincible but in openly engaging with life's messiness.

Authentic healing happens within compassionate communities and starts with openly discussing the challenges we all face.

Basking in Negative Reinforcement

In those comparison moments, a flood of anxiety, embarrassment, and even depression would overwhelm me and reinforce the belief that I was uniquely unqualified or defective somehow. Any mistake brought on a barrage of self-doubt and shame. The questions came like rapid fire.

- *How could I be so stupid?*
- *Why am I not better?*
- *Why am I not perfect?*
- *If only I were smarter.*
- *If only I were straight.*
- *If only I were better-looking.*
- *If only I lost weight.*
- *If only I had more money.*
- *If only I had the perfect partner.*
- *If only (fill in the blank), then everything would be perfect.*

Describe a time when things didn't unfold as you expected.

_____

_____

_____

What are the external factors you blame for your internal feelings or external circumstances?

_____

_____

_____

What have you told yourself in moments of self-doubt and shame? Which were truths, and which were self-limiting lies?

_____

_____

_____

These dangerous thoughts perpetuate a cycle of negative reinforcement, undermining our self-worth and preventing us from embracing our imperfections as part of our journey. Recognizing and challenging these destructive patterns is the first step toward fostering self-compassion and resilience. It's okay not to have all the answers or to stumble along the way.

Your worth is not defined by perfection but by your courage to face challenges head-on and grow from them.

As you continue your journey, remember that struggles are opportunities for growth, and every step taken with courage and self-compassion brings you closer to embracing your true potential.

Is the Hard Work Worth it?

———

Let's be real: Taking steps to dig deep and support yourself isn't easy! If it were, the world would likely look vastly different. What sets you apart is your willingness to unearth those painful spots and shine a light on the places you've been stuck.

There were many times when I felt giving up was the easier choice. Retreating into the familiar pain of navigating life's uncertainty felt safer. In reality, what defines us is the choice to face challenges head-on and persevere.

The good news is YOU ARE NOT ALONE.

Together, we are embarking on an introspective adventure that will challenge you to confront your truths, embrace your authenticity, and unlock your potential. This is not just another self-help book; it is a guide designed to help you finally get unstuck and move forward with your life.

The Honesty Report Card

At the core of the journey lies a powerful tool—the *Honesty Report Card*. This assessment is not merely a questionnaire; it is a mirror reflecting the deepest parts of your being, your aspirations, and the barriers that stand in your way. It offers a candid look at where you are right now and helps you map out a course for where you want to be.

To begin, simply scan the QR code that follows, and you will be taken directly to the *Honesty Report Card*. As you answer each question, remember there are no right or wrong answers. This is an assessment of where you are today. You will be able to revisit this *Honesty Report Card* anytime you like in order to see how new awareness may have shifted your responses. The goal is to be as open and authentic as possible, giving yourself the freedom to explore your true feelings, desires, and challenges.

This assessment is for you if you:
- Struggle with self-doubt and seek clarity.
- Feel stuck in your personal or professional life.
- Long for a deeper connection with yourself and others.
- Desire to understand your emotional triggers and responses.
- Are committed to personal growth and transformation.

How to engage with the *Honesty Report Card*:
1. **Find a Quiet Space.** Choose a comfortable, quiet place where you can reflect without interruptions. This is your time to focus on yourself.
2. **Be Honest.** Approach each question with honesty. The more truthful you are, the more insightful and helpful your results will be.
3. **Reflect on Your Answers.** Take your time to think about each question. Reflect on how you feel about your answers and what they reveal about you.
4. **Embrace Vulnerability.** This process may bring up emotions or realizations that are challenging. Embrace these moments as opportunities for growth and understanding.

To access the Honesty Report Card

Reflecting on Your Experience

Now that you've completed the *Honesty Report Card*, take a moment to review your experience.

This exercise was an invitation to examine the areas that have held you back from living the life you truly desire. It likely stirred some emotions that can serve as inspiration for taking your next steps. To put a fine point on this exercise, I invite you to consider the following:

Emotional Awareness. Did you feel relief, frustration, sadness, hope, or something else entirely? Recognizing these emotions is the first step towards understanding and addressing them.

_____

_____

_____

_____

New Insights. Which of your answers most surprised you? Sometimes, we uncover hidden truths about ourselves that we were previously unaware of. These insights can be powerful catalysts for change.

_____

_____

_____

_____

Actionable Steps: What areas of your life do you feel most compelled to work on after completing the assessment? Identifying these areas is crucial for setting meaningful goals and taking purposeful action.

_____

_____

_____

_____

Your journey doesn't end here. Use the insights and emotions brought to light by the *Honesty Report Card* as a foundation for the work you will do throughout this book. Allow these revelations to guide you as you navigate the path of self-discovery, healing, and growth.

Remember, the power to change and move forward lies within you. Embrace this journey with an open heart and mind, and let the *Honesty Report Card* be your compass, guiding you toward the life you truly deserve.

Here are a few reminders to support integrating what you've learned:

1. **Reflect Regularly.** Periodically revisit the *Honesty Report Card* to track your progress and reassess your current state.
2. **Seek Support.** Reach out to positive influences, mentors, or professional support to guide you through challenging areas.
3. **Stay Committed.** Consistently take small, intentional steps toward your goals, and maintain a mindset of growth and possibility.
4. **Practice Self-Compassion.** Continuously nurture yourself with love and understanding, especially during difficult times.

Unraveled

On that Halloween evening, I left Walmart empty-handed and returned home, only to go straight to bed. In this vulnerable state, I experienced an extraordinary dream, a vision that somehow stirred a renewed and unstoppable optimism within me.

As I awoke, the dream lingered, and I felt a burning determination to reclaim my place in the world. I was convinced that everything would be okay. I just needed to get up and get back to work. Work would be my salvation once again. My tried-and-true belief about work and success would serve as my escape hatch. I told myself it had worked before, and it would work again.

In an impulsive surge of energy, I took immediate action to symbolize my commitment to this change. I cut my hair, shaved, and dressed in proper clothes for the first time in months. With newfound enthusiasm coursing through my veins, I stepped out of the house, ready to actively contribute to this newest dream life of mine. Unfortunately, my real-world capabilities did not line up with my perceived breakthrough.

The following weeks were a whirlwind of frenetic activity to reclaim everything I had lost. It was a futile endeavor, like trying to rebuild a house on a broken foundation. I reconnected with old colleagues and searched for new business opportunities, ensuring that each day I showed up putting my best foot forward—or so I thought. In truth, it was complete chaos, and I was grasping at straws, trying to create some semblance of relevance that would help me reclaim my old life. I never paused to recognize or consider the state of my physical or mental well-being, leading to a deeper descent into the spiral that was already in motion. Each morning, I would don a mask of confidence, only to have it slip by midday, revealing the cracks in my facade. Meetings blurred into each other, conversations felt hollow, and the pressure of maintaining this charade was suffocating. My attempts at networking were frantic, filled with forced smiles and desperate pitches, all while my mind buzzed with unrelenting anxiety. Every night, I would collapse into bed, exhausted but unable to sleep, my mind racing with the fear of failure and the dread of another day of pretending.

Then, on a cold January day, everything screeched to an abrupt halt. I walked into the airport for a flight from Colorado to North Carolina. Without a confirmed seat, I was convinced my "confident and polished" presence alone would ensure my unused air miles were all I needed to execute my travel plans. The ticket agent did not share my steadfast commitment to that journey.

Driven by my sense of entitlement, shaky headspace, and self-importance, I dialed 911 at the airport. I was convinced the ticket agent was incompetent and that I was being wronged by not receiving a ticket using airline miles I believed I had. Surely, the police would help me right this injustice. My call quickly devolved into an escalated scene that was the final domino in my complete undoing.

The consequence of my hubris was lying face down near an airport check-in line, handcuffed, arrested, and later charged.

Until that fateful day, I'd never called 911, had never experienced police intervention outside of a traffic stop, and had never been in any kind of physical altercation.

I was not myself. I was completely undone.

In short order, my arrest led to the discovery of sizable hot checks—fraudulent checks written without sufficient funds to cover them—that I had recently written during a manic buying spree. To put this into context, this was a time when checks were still a common and acceptable form of payment, unlike today, where many people rely on certified bank checks to prevent such fraud. As my career was in real estate, most of these checks were written as earnest money for properties I believed I could afford to purchase. Completely detached from reality, I somehow concluded the money would magically appear in my account.

It didn't.

In an instant, my previously pristine record was permanently marred, transforming my private life into a sudden public spectacle. The repercussions of my poor choices crashed down on me with the unforgiving weight of the entire world. The stark reality was I could no longer escape the internal voices I had narrowly evaded until then. For someone who had fiercely guarded their privacy, I had been laid bare for an unkind world to scrutinize.

The devastation I experienced eclipsed any of my previous hardships. I found myself exposed and overwhelmed, facing an all-encompassing and inescapable grief. The isolation, which I had spent a lifetime trying to evade, hit me with unwavering force.

My decisions had brought me to my knees, and I wholeheartedly believed I deserved the hardship. At my lowest point, nothing else could have convinced me of the lessons I learned during that time. Despite kind words from others assuring me that "everyone makes mistakes," I couldn't bring myself to accept what it meant to be part of that collective "everyone."

This was much worse.

I had let others down.

I had let myself down.

I had failed at life.

I was a failure.

Discovering Freedom in Jail

My world had crumbled under the weight of regrettable choices, hurling me from privileged circles to a jail cell. In total, I spent seventy-two days behind bars. Every day, another misstep revealed that my reality was in stark contrast to the life I once thought I knew.

I naively assumed incarceration was reserved for others, not someone like me. However, jail is indifferent to one's pedigree, privilege, or success. For me, jail proved to be a great equalizer.

No possession or title could protect the vulnerable soul facing harsh realities. Stripped of my monetary armor, I was fully exposed, and the uncomfortable truths I had been avoiding—about self-worth, success, comparison, and superiority—now demanded my full attention.

My days were filled with interactions with incredibly complex characters. There was an aging businessman who was guilty of murdering his business partner and transporting his remains in the trunk of a Mercedes. A notorious con man who had swindled millions from his business partners yet offered legal advice to those willing to enrich his commissary. A former park ranger who had resorted to robbing a fast-food establishment after his life was ravished by a drug addiction.

Their stories were extraordinary, surpassing anything I had encountered in my own privileged circles. Yet, as I listened to their dramatic retelling of events, a crucial truth emerged: In jail, your identity, possessions, and past actions lose all significance. We were all equally wounded souls, navigating life's challenges within inescapable confinement. I was only different from the outside; our insides were much the same. We were full of shame, doubt, and blame.

Under the unforgiving fluorescent lights, illusions faded away. The only difference between us was the unique circumstances that brought us together. No institution can force courage or character; these qualities emerge from conscious choices. This fairly brief period of incarceration taught me that true freedom lies not in obtaining one's desires but in evolving into one's authentic self. The metaphorical bars only existed in the spaces where self-mastery was absent.

I entered jail as a man clinging to a frayed illusion of entitlement but emerged newly awakened to my sense of responsibility to myself.

Some Questions For You to Consider

These questions are designed to provoke deep introspection and encourage you to explore your own journey of self-discovery and growth, drawing insights from the narrative shared in the chapter. Take your time with each question, and allow yourself the space to uncover meaningful reflections that resonate with your personal experiences.

1. Recall a significant turning point in your life when you experienced a profound awakening. What sparked this pivotal moment? Describe the circumstances around that experience in detail.

_____

_____

_____

2. During times of personal crisis or intense challenges, what internal beliefs about yourself surfaced? What does your internal voice say to you? How did these beliefs influence your decisions?

_____

_____

_____

3. When has your perception of yourself clashed with reality? How did you navigate this realization, and what insights did you gain about resilience and self-discovery from that experience?

_____

_____

_____

Wherever You Go, There You Are

The aftermath of my experiences left me shattered, desperately seeking familiarity in the ruins of what once was. However, in the span of seventy-two days in jail, everything I held dear, specifically prestige and reputation, had completely vanished. The business persona had already evaporated. Now it seemed there was nothing left. I believed I couldn't begin again in the same place I'd come undone.

Thankfully, my parents supported my decision to start over in another state. My mom flew to Colorado to help me settle into a suburban extended-stay hotel. Room 320, a small studio, became my safe haven for the next year. Fortunately, my dad agreed to cover the weekly rent and my living expenses, providing the only sustainable lifeline I had.

In the blink of an eye, I abandoned all I had known and sought a fresh start where nothing was familiar. I believed this would be a solution, but regardless of the location, there I was. And despite the days, weeks, and months that passed, the normalcy I craved remained elusive. Escape from the abyss wasn't getting any easier. I found myself in deeper and darker places than ever before.

To cope during this excruciating time, I adopted a stance of detachment. I replayed each mistake as if I were a distant observer. I used every memory as an opportunity to cast judgment on my past self. I narrowed the sum total of my worth down to a single chapter of my life. By dismissing everything else, I allowed those specific instances to define my existence and perpetuate a damaging narrative that played on a loop in my mind.

For my first nine months in Colorado, I didn't have a car. As a lifelong car enthusiast, this was excruciating. I relied on my feet and public transportation to get around. I still have the black and yellow Sauconys that I am certain supported me at least 1,000 miles. I would often think about my eventual memoir, *Rolls Royce to Bus Pass.*

My daily walks were my only glimmer of hope. To start, I felt like I was battling through concrete, but I continued to put one foot in front of the other despite it all. Amidst my emotional highs and lows, I stared down considerable legal challenges, financial ruin, and continued poor mental health. I grappled with despair and pleaded to my higher power for release from the pain.

The Only Way Out is Through

A turning point came when my concerned mom suggested I join a local support peer group with others facing mental health struggles. My parents had recently participated in the National Alliance on Mental Illness's (NAMI) twelve-week Family-to-Family course, which prompted the thoughtful recommendation. Desperate and with no other viable alternatives in mind, I quickly found a nearby NAMI Connection peer support group.

Walking into that room one cold November evening, I planned to listen and learn, thinking I had nothing to lose. During the roundtable discussion among others struggling with mental health, I felt seen for the first time in a long time. While our stories differed, the welcoming and supportive atmosphere marked the beginning of a transformative journey. That NAMI Connection group became a cornerstone of my recovery, offering solace and connection that played a vital role in rebuilding my life.

I also began attending intensive weekly therapy sessions with an incredibly kind therapist who saw me pro bono for 18 months. Making those appointments required a long walk and two bus rides, but I was committed to finding relief from the constant pain and shame. For the first time in ages, I felt seen and heard. Each session was like a relief valve, easing my unrelenting negative thoughts.

She suggested I consider journaling to process and connect with what I was feeling. I was reluctant to do so, believing it would only unravel me further. However, daily journaling allowed me to process my grief and set realistic goals: making a call, paying a bill, taking a walk, or brushing my teeth. Completing a simple task became a milestone, affirming my progress and keeping me accountable for my future. Each step forward was a lifeline, pulling me back from the brink of despair.

It was crucial that I confront myself with brutal honesty amidst all of these small positive changes in my routine. With each action and the support of others, I traced my recent struggles back to childhood, gaining an understanding of their painful origins. I faced my fears and dismantled the walls I'd built to shield my fragile inner self. My struggles were not personal failings but an innate drive to survive my suffering in any way I could. This revelation marked a shift from automatic self-blame to mindful self-care. I learned that connection and people matter more than productivity and possessions.

For the first time, I cautiously opened up to others with complete transparency. Those I trusted responded with empathy, and many shared their own struggles in return. Mutual vulnerability demonstrated that speaking openly about adversity can foster profound connections.

Thanks to my newfound supportive connections, I found the courage to face the weight and consequences of my recent actions. Despite my steps toward healing, my life was still mired in legal challenges, decimated finances, and irreparably broken relationships. Reflecting on even one of these issues, let alone all of them, left me in a desperate state, searching for a way out.

I had to keep moving.

Step by step, I emerged from the depths of my despair. With each passing day, my commitment to showing up for others grew stronger. I began volunteering at a nearby library and became a trained facilitator for the NAMI support group that had played such a pivotal role in my own recovery. Eventually, I became a valued member of the NAMI affiliate board and eventually took on its first paid President and CEO role.

This, Too, Shall Pass

Five years passed in the blink of an eye, and my life looked radically different. While challenges persisted, I gained new tools and a fresh perspective on how to navigate them. In fairness, some days were tough, but I showed up with radical self-compassion and a steadfast belief that "this, too, shall pass."

Today, my passion lies in bolstering those currently navigating parallel struggles of their own. In supporting others, I recognize echoes of my own journey and embrace the opportunity to extend empathy, hope, and practical guidance. Through my trials, I unearthed purpose and significance that eclipsed the superficial triumphs of the past I left behind.

This journey taught me a vital lesson: Moving to a new place won't solve your problems if you don't also work on healing yourself. Changing your environment can help, but true transformation comes from within. It requires facing your past, understanding your struggles, and embracing the support of those around you. This combination of internal and external change is what ultimately led to my growth and a renewed sense of self.

Seeing Your Reflection

We've all heard someone say, "I don't want to go to therapy because there's no point in dwelling on the past." Maybe you've even felt this way yourself. In my own journey, I realized my relentless pursuit of perfection and my habit of putting others' needs ahead of my own were deeply rooted in unresolved trauma from my past. These patterns kept me stuck, unable to fully embrace the life I desired.

I learned firsthand that moving forward required confronting my past, including my perfectionism and tendency to overextend myself for others. It was only when I faced these truths head-on, with compassion and courage, that I began to break free from the cycle of self-sabotage.

It's understandable to feel hesitant about digging into the past. The idea of revisiting old wounds can be daunting, and the fear of uncovering painful memories can hold you back. Yet, acknowledging and understanding these parts of yourself is crucial for true growth and healing.

By looking at your past, you might uncover similar patterns or beliefs that have shaped your actions and decisions. Perhaps you'll recognize the fear of failure that's kept you from taking risks or the need for external validation that's driven you to overextend yourself. These revelations can be uncomfortable, but they are also incredibly empowering. They provide the clarity needed to make conscious choices that align with your true self.

It's a chance to understand how your past experiences have influenced your present reality and to use that insight as a foundation for change. The emotions that arise during this process—whether it's sadness, anger, fear, or even relief—are signals that you're tapping into something significant. Allow yourself to feel these emotions fully, and use them as fuel for your journey forward. Recognize that every step you take in exploring these aspects of yourself is a courageous act of self-love. It's a testament to your resilience and your commitment to living a more authentic and fulfilling life.

By choosing to take a more introspective look at yourself, you're making a powerful statement that you are ready to face whatever has been holding you back and that you believe in your ability to create the life you truly desire. Embrace this opportunity with an open heart, knowing that the strength and clarity you gain will guide you toward a brighter future.

What past experiences are most vivid in your memory?

_____

_____

_____

What feelings arise as you reflect on how those past experiences have shaped your actions and decisions?

_____

_____

_____

Confronting Childhood Shadows

In 1985, Dr. Vincent Felitti, head of Kaiser Permanente's groundbreaking Department of Preventive Medicine in San Diego, California, was baffled by the consistent dropout rate exceeding fifty percent annually in his obesity clinic for five consecutive years. This mystery set the stage for a twenty-five-year investigation that involved researchers from the Centers for Disease Control and Prevention and more than 17,000 members of Kaiser Permanente's San Diego program.

The inquiry uncovered the startling revelation that adverse experiences during childhood were remarkably prevalent, even among the white, middle-class population. Furthermore, these experiences were also linked to nearly every major chronic illness and societal challenge faced by citizens in the United States, incurring billions of dollars annually.

The study, known as ACEs (Adverse Childhood Experiences), proposed that ten specific adverse childhood experiences can serve as predictors for subsequent health and social repercussions. Researchers delved into the relationships between ten ACEs, including:

- Child physical abuse
- Child sexual abuse
- Child emotional abuse
- Emotional neglect
- Physical neglect
- Mentally ill, depressed, or suicidal person in the home

- Drug-addicted or alcoholic family member
- Witnessing domestic violence against the mother
- Loss of a parent to death or abandonment by parental divorce
- Incarceration of any family member for a crime

This comprehensive exploration shed light on the profound impact of early experiences on long-term well-being, emphasizing the critical need to understand and address these factors for true healing and growth. For deeper work, professional therapy may be essential, offering a structured environment to process and integrate these experiences for lasting change.

I experienced nine of these factors: my childhood was filled with alcoholism, emotional and sexual abuse, bullying, divorced and emotionally absent parents, and a mother who was continually emotionally abused by my stepfather. Each factor contributed to an unpredictable inner life that left me constantly on edge, hyper-aware of the moods of those around me.

The Hidden Cost of Perfectionism and People-Pleasing

Experiencing 9 of the ACE factors, my childhood was anything but protective. My tendency to be a people-pleaser—always prepared, eager to help, and perpetually overworked did lead to my eventual financial success in adulthood. However, this also meant I hid a deep emotional void, avoiding close relationships and emotional intimacy.

While these adaptive traits propelled me toward financial success, they also obscured a profound sense of inadequacy and unworthiness that constantly troubled me. I became skilled at concealing this deep insecurity, burying it under layers of tasks and responsibilities.

My constant need to please others and maintain appearances became a barrier to forming meaningful relationships and experiencing genuine emotional connection. I became hyper-focused on how everything looked, believing that if my outer world seemed "perfect," no one would see the brokenness I felt inside. It felt safer to keep everyone at a distance, avoiding the vulnerability of sharing my inner struggles. Despite appearing successful on the outside, I battled with feelings of inadequacy, constantly fearing that if people truly knew me, they would uncover the emptiness I worked so hard to hide.

We are taught that external things can fill internal voids, but time and again, this proves to be a hollow promise. The illusion that prosperity can resolve the core aspects of human existence—introspection, self-discovery, and emotional healing—fails to deliver true fulfillment.

I hid my internal shame and fear behind smiles and small talk. I ensured conversations were superficial. As a result, I made my needs secondary and assumed no one felt them (or me) important. When asked about myself, I was an expert at redirecting the questions back to others, thereby accomplishing two things: never being vulnerable and maintaining my image as an altruist. Friends have mused, "You know everything about me, and I know so little about you." I had mastered the art of deflection.

In navigating my wreckage, I uncovered that abundance meant little without a willingness to confront my flaws. The journey toward wholeness required a courageous confrontation of the shadows of the past, unearthing a lifetime of traumas, and embracing authenticity. It was time I stood face-to-face with my demons.

As I peered inward, I realized the pursuit of unattainable perfection had exacted a heavy toll on my life. It had robbed me of real authenticity, which I could only experience through vulnerability, acknowledging my imperfections, confronting pain, and embracing the entirety of my being.

If there were an *Honesty Report Card* for my early years, it would have been a sobering reflection of a tumultuous childhood marked by considerable pain and challenge. Growing up amidst alcoholism, emotional and sexual abuse, bullying, and parental absence, alongside a mother facing constant emotional abuse, created a turbulent environment. Despite outward success driven by perfectionism and people-pleasing, this facade had masked deep emotional wounds and a profound sense of unworthiness. Avoiding vulnerability became a survival strategy, keeping me from authentic connections and leaving me isolated despite outward achievements.

PART II
Turning Setbacks Into Strength

Value of Being Vulnerable

In a world that often celebrates strength and resilience, vulnerability is frequently viewed as a weakness to be avoided at all costs. However, we will explore a profound truth: vulnerability is not a liability but a gateway to profound transformation and personal growth.

Since Brené Brown's TED Talk on shame and vulnerability went viral in 2010, vulnerability has become a buzzword in therapeutic and self-help circles. But what does it actually feel like to be vulnerable rather than just talk about it? Being vulnerable means fully trusting something outside our own mind to admit our scariest and darkest fears.

Whether you are journaling a detailed account of your childhood abuse or sharing that story with a therapist or friend, practicing vulnerability can be a slow and daunting process. However, once we expose all the corners of our minds, we unlock a new freedom unlike any other.

Vulnerability is the courageous act of allowing ourselves to be seen, truly seen, with all our imperfections and insecurities laid bare. It requires us to step out of the safety of our comfort zones and into the unknown, where the magic of transformation awaits.

At its core, vulnerability is about authenticity—the willingness to show up and be real, even when it's uncomfortable or scary. It's about acknowledging our fears, doubts, and struggles without shame or judgment and embracing them as integral parts of our human experience.

But why is vulnerability so transformative? Because it opens the door to connection, empathy, and resilience in ways that nothing else can. When we allow ourselves to be vulnerable, we invite others to do the same, fostering deep and meaningful connections that enrich our lives immeasurably.

Vulnerability is the birthplace of creativity, innovation, and personal breakthroughs. It is in our moments of vulnerability that we discover our true strength and potential as we confront our fears head-on and emerge stronger and more resilient on the other side.

Think of vulnerability as the soil in which seeds of transformation are planted. It is only by tilling the soil, pulling out the weeds, exposing the seeds to the elements, and nurturing them with care and compassion that new seeds can take root and blossom into something beautiful.

Embracing vulnerability is not always easy. It requires courage, resilience, and a willingness to lean into discomfort. It means letting go of the need to control every outcome and surrendering to the unpredictable nature of life.

Yet, the rewards of vulnerability are immeasurable. It is through vulnerability that we discover our true selves, forge deeper connections with others, and unleash our full potential. It is the key that unlocks the door to a life of authenticity, purpose, and fulfillment.

So, I invite you to view vulnerability as your greatest ally on the journey of transformation. Allow yourself to be seen, to be heard, and to be truly known. See your imperfections and vulnerabilities as gifts, not flaws, and watch as they become the catalysts for profound growth and change in your life. As you take the next step, remember these words:

> *"Vulnerability is not a sign of weakness, but the greatest measure of courage. It is the willingness to show up and be seen, even when there are no guarantees. And it is through vulnerability that we discover the true depth of our strength and resilience."*

In my experience as a public speaker and facilitator, I'm always amazed at how others open up and share their deeply personal stories after I've shared mine. It reaffirms the power of connection through shared struggle. While our individual stories are unique, the common points where we get stuck become opportunities for meaningful connection. It serves as an affirmation of how we are all interconnected through our individual experiences.

Navigating life's challenges can feel like standing at the bottom of a daunting staircase, unsure of how to reach the top. My "next right step" approach is about focusing on one step at a time, understanding this is the only way to climb higher. This approach emphasizes the power of incremental progress, encouraging you to take manageable actions rather than becoming overwhelmed by the entire journey.

In the coming pages, you'll find reflection questions designed to support you in identifying and taking your next right step. These questions are intended to guide you through each phase of your journey, helping you to move forward with confidence and clarity.

Take Your Next Right Step

How has your fear of vulnerability impacted your relationships and personal growth? Reflect on instances where you held back from showing your true self. How did it affect your connection with others and your ability to grow?

_____

_____

_____

In what areas of your life could embracing vulnerability lead to transformative change? Consider the parts of your life where you resist being open. How might embracing vulnerability in these areas unlock new opportunities for connection and personal breakthroughs?

_____

_____

_____

Facing Our Fears Head-on

Struggle Does Not Define Your Worthiness

Struggles are the rough places that prepare us for growth. They are evidence of our purpose, waiting to be uncovered. When we face difficulties without fear, each challenge prepares us for a deeper understanding of the world around us. In these shared truths, we find connection, allowing everything else to start falling into place.

Beginning again after my own catastrophic losses revealed that we all struggle with self-doubt, anxiety, relationships, and overall purpose. Despite these universal struggles, most of us still suffer silently until the pain is unbearable or until it seems too late to even try to change. We belong to a society that is quick to label imperfections as weaknesses and teaches us to be afraid to admit failure.

Several fateful events that happened in quick succession shook my core. They forced me to acknowledge how long I had repressed my authentic needs and emotions and that I could no longer outrun myself. It wasn't until the deeply painful collapse of my life that I slowly found the courage to open up and become authentically whole. At rock bottom, I was out of options, and continuing to hide was too painful.

Breaking a self-imposed isolation by giving voice to my truth shifted my mindset from feeling defective to being connected. I began prioritizing self-care over productivity and community over competition.

Integrating steps towards vulnerability and moving beyond secrecy, I slowly transitioned from hiding to openness. Today, committing to this shared human experience serves as a crucial anchor and mirror, reminding me that we all navigate a winding path filled with occasional stumbles. On days when anxiety over achievement threatens my progress, witnessing others lovingly navigate life's ups and downs restores my balance. The personal lessons we exchange along the way nourish roots strong enough to weather all of life's storms.

In the upcoming pages of this book, I'll provide some practical tools to reframe the common battles we face in order to make them less intimidating. The crucial first step is recognizing that everyone walks this path with an inescapable amount of collateral damage.

Let this truth resonate: you're not alone, and there is hope when we join hands as comrades rather than competitors.

Walk with courage, not fear. Progress awaits, but we have to take it step by step. You've already begun the journey by turning this page and taking steps to embrace self-acceptance. Now, it's time to start shifting your perspective.

Growth Requires Action

Begin by selecting a specific fear that you feel comfortable exploring. Go deep to confront something that has significantly held you back or hindered your progress. Often, these fears are closely tied to our anxiety about losing control. Suffering usually stems from imagining worst-case scenarios that rarely come to pass. Think about it—how often do you ruminate on an outcome that never actually happens as you envision? For me, it's nearly 100 percent of the time. With this in mind, identify your core fear and challenge yourself by asking, *What if something different happened?*

Next, extend compassion to the origin of your struggle, whether it stems from old wounds, societal conditioning, or generational survival patterns you've integrated into your daily habits. If you find it difficult to access compassion for yourself, imagine a loved one coming to you for help with the same issue. This step is about learning to be kind to yourself. While society often celebrates victories, true personal growth arises from navigating the messy middle.

Finally, redefine your struggles as stepping stones toward a clearer purpose. Although obstacles may seem insurmountable up close, life's journey extends far beyond our immediate view. Keep moving one foot forward, and remember that everything you need is already within you.

- **Recognize and Acknowledge Your Fears.** Begin by acknowledging your fears. Write them down and give them names. This act alone can diminish their power over you.
- **Analyze the Root Cause.** Understand where these fears come from. Are they based on past experiences, societal expectations, or inherited beliefs? This reflection can help you see your fears in a new light.
- **Extend Compassion to Yourself.** Show yourself kindness and patience. Think about how you would support a loved one facing the same fears. Apply that same compassion to yourself.
- **Challenge Negative Thoughts.** When you catch yourself imagining worst-case scenarios, ask, *What if something different happened?* Challenge your fears by envisioning positive outcomes.
- **Take Small Steps Forward.** Face your fears in manageable steps. Celebrate each small victory along the way. These small steps will build your confidence and resilience.

- **Redefine Your Struggles.** See your challenges as opportunities for growth rather than obstacles. Every struggle is a lesson that can guide you toward a clearer purpose.

Life's journey extends beyond our immediate view, and sometimes, the path is obscured. Keep moving forward, even when it feels difficult. Remember that stumbling is part of the process, and every step you take brings you closer to the light. It's your time to embrace the transformative power of vulnerability.

Take Your Next Right Step

What small step can you take today to face your fears and move forward?

_____

_____

_____

How can you show yourself compassion as you navigate your struggles?

_____

_____

_____

By continuously striving to rise toward the light, we support each other in our journeys, transforming our fears into stepping stones for personal growth and fulfillment.

Vulnerability Leads to Authenticity

Embracing the transformative power of vulnerability is your next step toward growth and self-discovery. Consider the challenges you currently face and observe the emotions they evoke. As you thoughtfully reflect on these struggles, notice any self-doubt that arises and gently address yourself with the same compassion you would offer a loved one. This simple yet powerful exercise helps shift your perspective from feeling personally defective to recognizing that struggle is a universal part of the human experience. Think about how your fear of vulnerability has impacted your relationships and personal growth.

Engage in a reflective practice where you acknowledge your self-doubts without judgment, understanding they are natural aspects of being human. Speak kindly to yourself, just as you would to a friend facing similar doubts. This intentional act of self-compassion can reframe your internal dialogue and foster kindness towards yourself instead of harsh self-criticism.

To illustrate the power of vulnerability, let me share a personal story. I've struggled with mental health issues for a lot of my life, and the shame that accompanied these struggles often felt insurmountable. While it was easier to be open with those who understood, meeting new people or interacting with those outside my circle filled me with near-crippling anxiety. This was especially true when I was dating. It always felt like a delicate dance of when and how to share my story, usually revealing it in chapters over time.

When I met my partner, Gus, I knew I wanted to be honest about my history with openness and vulnerability. He felt safe, and I felt the walls of shame come down. Each time I would dip my toe in the water with new details, he would meet me at that place with kindness and empathy. With time, other details of my story would emerge, ones I thought I had already shared. We would laugh when he said, "You didn't tell me that story." I hadn't intended to be exclusionary, but I was so used to glossing over the fine points for fear of judgment from others.

This experience taught me that you will meet people along the way who will meet you right where you are and love you for every experience that makes you uniquely you. By being vulnerable and sharing my true self, I was able to build a deeper, more authentic connection with my partner. This not only strengthened our relationship but also helped me see that vulnerability is a pathway to genuine connection and self-acceptance.

By doing so, you are taking steps toward self-discovery and connection. Recognize that moments of struggle and self-doubt are not signs of personal inadequacy but shared human experiences. This shift in perspective creates a sense of solidarity with others, reminding you that imperfection is a natural part of being human. Through self-compassion and reframing your struggles, you cultivate resilience and inner strength, empowering you to face life's challenges with greater ease and grace.

Take Your Next Right Step

Write about a challenge you are currently facing.

_____

_____

_____

What emotions does this challenge evoke?

_____

_____

_____

In what areas of your life could embracing vulnerability lead to change?

_____

_____

_____

Breakdowns Lead to Breakthroughs

For nearly a decade, I felt overpowering waves of shame and regret wash over me as I relived my greatest failures. My inner critic hurled accusations, confirming what I'd secretly feared all along: I'm not good enough. I believed those mistakes proved my character was irreparably flawed.

My history is characterized by a habit of putting myself last, thanks to an innate desire to serve others and meet their needs first. Doing so left me feeling drained and resentful.

Every action has both a light and a dark side. On the light side, I aimed to be helpful, generous, and fully committed to providing support to others. But the shadow aspect of my behavior stemmed from my drive to present myself as "good enough," hoping that would externally outweigh any perceived shortcomings one might attribute to me. I now recognize this perspective was not firmly grounded in reality, as most individuals are primarily engrossed in their own understanding of a situation.

Others' perception of us is their story, not ours.

Breaking Free From the Chains of Self-Sacrifice

Self-sacrifice was a recurring pattern in my life, deeply woven into my daily existence from an early age. This was evident in my work supporting others in a mental health non-profit. There was always a need from those struggling, allowing me to hide behind their stories.

Outwardly, I dedicated myself to attending to the needs and desires of those around me, readily offering my time, energy, and resources without hesitation. Despite my apparent generosity and selflessness, I grappled with an overwhelming sense of emptiness and discontent.

Each act of self-sacrifice seemed to fill a void within me, one that expanded with every gesture of giving. No matter how much I poured into serving others, the emptiness remained insatiable, its hunger growing stronger each day. At first, I mistook this emptiness as penance for my past mistakes or a noble sacrifice, believing that prioritizing others' needs above my own was a testament to my compassion. However, over time, I recognized a darker truth.

Self-sacrifice had become a convenient way to avoid confronting my own fears, insecurities, and uncertainties. By immersing myself in others' needs, I found temporary refuge from the daunting task of introspection and personal growth. It was easier to lose myself in service than to face the challenges of evolving and taking chances on myself.

With this new awareness, I dug deeper into this pattern and realized the toll it was taking on my well-being and fulfillment. The more I sacrificed myself, the further I drifted from my dreams, desires, and aspirations. By sacrificing my own needs on the altar of selflessness, I was inadvertently robbing myself of a chance at true happiness and self-fulfillment.

I learned to recognize this pattern of self-sacrifice was deeply rooted in my relationship with my mother. A strong and accomplished woman, she rose to the heights of her career despite being overshadowed by my stepfather, an alcoholic and narcissistic bully. For years, I took on the role of emotionally supporting her, believing it was my responsibility, even at my own peril. I was a confidante, trying to shield her from the emotional abuse and instability that permeated our home. This role of emotional caretaking bled into other areas of my life, reinforcing the belief that my worth was tied to how much I could give to others.

Slowly, I began to recognize that sustainable growth and fulfillment couldn't be achieved through self-sacrifice alone. It required confronting my inner demons, embracing vulnerability, and taking chances on myself, even in the face of uncertainty and discomfort. With a lot of deep work and understanding, I realized this pattern of supporting her was never my role. We each have our own lessons to learn, and while others may make the process easier, the work is ours to do alone.

To this day, I strive to break free from the chains of self-sacrifice, reclaim ownership of my narrative, and pursue a path of self-discovery and personal evolution. Only by daring to take chances on me can I truly find the fulfillment and purpose I seek beyond the hollow promises of self-sacrifice. With practice, this becomes more automatic. When I slip backward, I quickly recognize and adjust old patterns.

It took years to realize that my pattern of self-sacrifice and self-deprecation was unsustainable. The emptiness within me, once dismissed as a byproduct of my giving nature, could no longer be ignored. So, I embarked on a journey of self-discovery, determined to rewrite the narrative that had imprisoned me for too long. If this mindset sounds familiar, please know that self-blame serves no one—especially not you. It locks us in destructive cycles that block growth, fuel isolation, and corrode self-worth. This was my reality until a powerful revelation changed how I viewed failure and navigated challenges.

What if, regardless of any missteps, you deserve love, belonging, and joy right now?

By acknowledging this truth, I learned that true selflessness involves taking care of oneself first, enabling us to genuinely support others without losing our own identity and well-being.

If I Hadn't Been There, I Wouldn't Be Here

For years, I was trapped in a cycle of self-criticism, reliving my most painful moments daily. I believed I deserved every hurtful experience, despite positive self-talk and deep self-work. A nagging inner critic constantly told me I brought it all on myself.

This cycle wasn't truly revealed until quite recently when I appeared as a guest on a podcast. The interviewer's question planted a seed in my mind, suggesting that my struggles had shaped me into the person meant to do the work I do today. This was a profound realization that felt like a weight lifted from my shoulders. I breathed. Finally, this awareness felt like permission to stop replaying the painful tape from a relatively short period in a long life. This new understanding finally brought the bigger picture into focus. For years, I hated the experiences that had shaped me into someone committed to serving others. It was because of my story that I could authentically show up in service.

Despite what your inner voice may say, you are already whole, just as you are. Your current struggles or failures do not diminish your humanity or determine your capacity to make a meaningful impact. In fact, your struggles are the stories that have shaped you into the beautiful creation you are—and will continue to be.

A bad chapter doesn't equal a bad life.

Self-compassion requires seeing ourselves exactly as we are without attacking what we lack. It means releasing regret over the past and anxiety about the future, as worthiness is found only in the present moment. It's human to love yourself even after making mistakes and facing seemingly insurmountable hardships.

That nagging inner critic may still rise up, trying to convince you otherwise. Instead, treat it like a well-intentioned but misguided friend—kindly thank it for trying to keep you in check, then set clear boundaries against its toxicity. Actively pivot your inner dialogue from self-judgment to self-encouragement.

Take Your Next Right Step

Reflect on self-sacrifice. Take a moment to think about times when you put others before yourself. How did it make you feel?

_____

_____

_____

_____

_____

Question negative thoughts. Challenge any thoughts that make you feel unworthy or that cause you to blame yourself. Are they helping you grow?

_____

_____

_____

_____

Learn from your past. See your past mistakes and challenges as parts of your journey. Understand that they've shaped the strong person you are today. What past challenge makes you feel strong today?

_____

_____

_____

_____

Focus on the now. Your worth is determined by this moment. Let go of regrets and future worries, and embrace where you are now. Describe one action you can take today to get unstuck. Depending on where you are, it can be as simple as making your bed or starting that book you always wanted to write.

_____

_____

_____

Exercise daily self-kindness. Make daily efforts to be kind to yourself. Use affirmations, mindfulness, or self-care practices. Build a habit of self-compassion.

_____

_____

_____

_____

Remember, it's about the small steps you take each day. You deserve love and kindness, which begins by giving it to yourself.

Take The Next Right Step

In the pursuit of our dreams, the overwhelming pressure to make multiple and significant changes quickly can leave us paralyzed. We find ourselves stuck in an endless loop of "shoulds" and "coulds," unsure of where to begin or pick back up if we've left off. Here, we explore the value of taking small, manageable steps toward the life you desire.

> *A journey of gradual transformation starts with a single step; the only way we get up any staircase is by taking one step at a time.*

Overcome Resistance to Taking Small Steps

When we're overwhelmed, we resist taking small steps, believing that only significant changes can make a difference. A fear of inadequacy can paralyze us, but the key to progress lies in commitment and consistency. Instead of aiming for drastic changes, choose steps you can confidently commit to.

For instance, when I decided to improve my physical health, overhauling my entire lifestyle felt daunting. I spent months imagining myself healthier and more fit, but that alone wasn't enough to get me moving. It took a reboot of my mindset to realize that even the smallest step toward my goal was still a step. I started with a manageable step I could commit to: walking for 15 minutes each day. By sticking to this simple routine, I gradually built up my stamina and confidence, eventually incorporating more extensive exercise and healthier eating habits into my life. This consistent, small effort led to significant, lasting change over time.

All-or-nothing thinking can trap us in inaction. Recognize the value of small steps and acknowledge that progress, no matter how incremental, always matters. When I first wanted to write a book, the sheer scale of the project overwhelmed me. For quite some time, my old fear of not being perfect paralyzed me. Instead of giving up, I started by committing to write one paragraph each day. Eventually, I set a goal of one page, then two. This simple, manageable goal kept me moving forward, and over time, those pages added up to an entire manuscript. Each completed page was a small victory that motivated me to keep going, proving that even incremental progress is valuable.

Regain Direction by Taking the Next Right Step

Reflecting on my own life's twists and turns, I found myself underemployed and earnestly dedicating my energy to the service of others while unintentionally neglecting my own needs. I was constantly volunteering for community events, assisting friends and family with their problems, and always being available to lend a helping hand. I spent long hours supporting others' dreams and crises, ignoring my own rest and personal aspirations. My own needs were pushed to the background, leaving me feeling drained and unfulfilled.

During this poignant season of service to others, I attempted to focus more on taking the "next right step" for me, regardless of how big or small. Though my personal trials were difficult, I can now recognize they were instrumental in shaping the person I became. It was through these hardships that I made a heartfelt commitment to not only serve others but also to prioritize my well-being.

Boundaries are a way to love not only ourselves but also to build trust with others.

In the journey of personal growth and self-discovery, it is easy to become overwhelmed by the magnitude of our aspirations and the challenges that lie ahead. Whether we are striving to overcome addiction, healing from past traumas, or simply seeking to better ourselves, the path can seem daunting. This is where the wisdom of taking the next right step comes into play—a powerful approach rooted in various philosophies and practices that helps us navigate our journey one manageable step at a time.

The Power of Small Steps

Imagine you are at the base of a mountain, looking up at its towering peak. The distance to the top can feel insurmountable. But what if, instead of focusing on the peak, you concentrated solely on the next step in front of you? By shifting your focus to the immediate, the journey becomes less intimidating and more attainable. This is the essence of taking the next right step—focusing on what you can do right now to move forward.

"Take the next right step" has become my mantra. It is a concept widely discussed in contexts of self-help, recovery, and personal development. It emphasizes focusing on the immediate next action that aligns with one's goals or values rather than becoming overwhelmed by the larger picture. This idea has roots in various philosophies and practices:

- **12-Step Programs.** In Alcoholics Anonymous (AA) and other 12-step programs, participants are encouraged to focus on taking life "one day at a time" and making progress through small, manageable steps. This approach helps individuals avoid feeling overwhelmed by their long-term recovery journey.
- **Mindfulness and Present-Moment Awareness.** Mindfulness practices, rooted in Buddhist traditions and popularized in the West through figures like Jon Kabat-Zinn, emphasize living in the present moment. This includes making conscious choices about the immediate next step rather than getting lost in worries about the future or regrets about the past.
- **Stephen R. Covey's *The 7 Habits of Highly Effective People*.** Covey's work encourages individuals to "put first things first" and focus on what is most important and immediate. This principle aligns with the idea of taking the next right step.
- **Christian Faith and Guidance.** Many Christians follow the idea of seeking guidance for the "next right thing" in their daily lives based on teachings from the Bible and spiritual discernment.

- **General Psychological Approaches.** Cognitive Behavioral Therapy (CBT) and other therapeutic methods often advise breaking down larger goals into smaller, achievable actions. This helps individuals make consistent progress without becoming overwhelmed.

These sources collectively contribute to the widespread adoption and application of the "take the next right step" philosophy.

This mantra has helped me navigate life's complexities with purpose and resilience. Through deliberate actions, I rebuilt the foundation of my existence. Every action served as a testament to the profound impact that small, focused steps can have on one's journey and showcased my dedication to incremental progress, which can lead to the construction of a more fulfilling life.

Applying the Approach

Taking the next right step requires a blend of mindfulness, intentionality, and trust. It begins with a clear understanding of your goals and values, followed by a commitment to focus on immediate actions that align with them. Here are some practical steps to apply this approach:

1. **Clarify Your Vision.** Take time to reflect on your long-term goals and aspirations. What is it that you truly want to achieve? Write it down and keep it somewhere visible.
2. **Identify the Immediate Action.** Break down your larger goals into smaller, manageable steps. What is the one thing you can do right now that will move you closer to your goal?
3. **Take Action.** Focus on the present moment and take the next step. It might be a small action, but it is a step forward.
4. **Reflect and Adjust.** After taking action, reflect on the outcome. Did it bring you closer to your goal? If not, adjust your approach and identify the next right step.

5. **Practice Consistency.** Consistency is key. By regularly taking small, purposeful steps, you build momentum and make steady progress toward your goals.

In my own journey, the practice of taking the next right step has been transformative. During my darkest moments, when the path forward seemed unclear, this approach provided a sense of direction and purpose. It taught me to trust the process, to have faith in my ability to navigate challenges, and to recognize the power of small, consistent actions.

For instance, during my time as the interim Executive Director of a non-profit, I faced significant challenges and felt undervalued. Instead of succumbing to despair, I used journaling to process my emotions and gain clarity. By focusing on the next right step, I was able to reassess my goals, develop new skills, and ultimately chart a course toward a more fulfilling career path aligned with my values and aspirations.

Take Your Next Right Step

As you embark on your own journey of self-discovery and growth, I encourage you to embrace the practice of taking the next right step. Reflect on the following questions:

What unhealed wounds from your past continue to influence your present behaviors, emotions, and relationships? Reflect on the stories you have buried and consider how they might be manifesting in your daily life.

_____

_____

_____

During your darkest moments, what hidden strengths and resilience have you discovered within yourself? Think about how you have navigated challenges and what personal growth emerged from those experiences.

_____

_____

_____

How have your hardships clarified your values and priorities? Ask yourself, "How did this hardship clarify what matters most to me?" and explore how these realizations have shaped your path.

_____

_____

_____

What practices, such as journaling or meditation, have helped you process your emotions and find meaning in difficult experiences? Reflect on the tools and methods you have used to navigate through pain and how they have contributed to your personal growth.

_____

_____

_____

By focusing on the next right step, you can navigate your journey with greater clarity, purpose, and resilience. Each small step brings you closer to your goals, transforming challenges into opportunities for growth and self-discovery.

Checking Your Inner Critic

Freeing yourself of past pain or worry about the future is challenging work. But on this journey, you never walk alone. Countless others know this path, and all of our stories connect us rather than separate us. An inheritance gifted to us at birth cannot be bought, bargained for, or lost, no matter how much difficulty one faces.

What helped me tremendously was giving my inner critic a voice and entering into healthy dialogue in order to redefine our relationship. I acknowledged driving forces from my past that made the voice initially feel necessary. Then I set clear intentions on how to move forward with compassion, not criticism that corroded my spirit.

It takes daily practice, but the inner voice eventually settles with the realization that no matter what hardship one must pass through, it is inherently worthwhile.

You have always been and will always be profoundly worthy, just as you are right now.

Let this truth settle gently into your whole being.

Replace Your Inner Critic with a Voice of Worthiness

Imagine a scenario where you're presented with a golden opportunity in your career: a chance to lead a high-profile project that aligns perfectly with your skills. Excitement surges through you, but then that inner critic begins to whisper doubt and insecurity.

The voice tells you that you're not qualified, that you'll inevitably fail, and that everyone around you will soon realize you're an imposter. As these thoughts intensify, anxiety sets in, and you find yourself hesitating to rise to the occasion.

This internal dialogue can be the most powerful determinant of whether or not you take action. If you succumb to negativity, you might decline the opportunity and miss out on a chance for growth and success. Fueled by your inner critic, imposter syndrome prevents you from realizing your full potential.

However, with self-awareness and intentional effort, you can learn to successfully navigate ups and downs. Instead of letting the negative voice control your actions, you can replace it with an empowered one. In this example, you might start by acknowledging you are qualified for the opportunity, recognizing your skills and achievements, and understanding that everyone faces challenges. Remember, those encouraging you to take on more responsibilities likely already have confidence in your abilities.

The power to rewrite your story lies within you. You have the pen, and your story is worth telling. The anecdotes shared in this book can be used as mirrors reflecting the resilience and worthiness within each of us. Embrace the truth that your journey, with all of its struggles and triumphs, is uniquely yours and profoundly valuable.

With your newfound insight, take the next right step toward radical self-acceptance. Challenge the narratives that limit your potential, replace doubt with empowerment, and embark on the trajectory of intentional action. Your story is still unfolding, and every choice you make contributes to your strength, purpose, and boundless worth.

Seeking Constructive Feedback From Supportive Relationships

Seeking insights and feedback from those who can offer it constructively and know when to hold their tongues can significantly assist in your self-discovery and growth.

Surround yourself with people who have true insights about what you'd like to accomplish. Those who understand the value of constructive criticism and possess the empathy to offer feedback in a supportive manner. These individuals recognize their role is not to tear you down but to help you build yourself up, offering insights and perspectives that can guide you toward your goals.

In my life, I've been fortunate to have others play pivotal roles in my personal and professional development. For instance, a mentor who provided thoughtful feedback on my writing helped me refine my skills and grow as a communicator. Their feedback wasn't focused on tearing apart my work but rather on identifying areas for improvement and offering guidance on how to address them.

Similarly, friends who possess a keen sense of empathy and understanding are invaluable sources of support during challenging times. Their ability to listen with compassion and provide constructive insights helps them navigate difficult situations to gain clarity on the path forward.

When seeking feedback, it's essential to be discerning about who you invite into that process. Look for individuals who have your best interests at heart, who possess the expertise or experience to offer valuable insights, and who approach feedback with empathy and kindness. By surrounding yourself with such individuals, you can cultivate a supportive environment that fosters growth, resilience, and self-discovery.

If you're uncertain about how to approach a new challenge, the worst thing you can do for your self-confidence and energy is to seek advice and approval from someone who talks excessively, lacks knowledge of your struggle, and pressures you to follow their advice. Instead, trust your gut and focus on seeking guidance from trusted resources who listen with empathy, compassion, and concern for your highest and best outcome. Check in with yourself. You likely have had a nagging feeling for some time about what feels right—honor that intuition as a valuable guide.

Now, with constructive feedback, you can intentionally reframe your narrative with words of self-empowerment and kindness. Affirm your own worthiness and capability, recognizing that imperfection is a shared human experience.

Commit to a daily practice of self-compassion, gently guiding your inner dialogue toward statements of encouragement and understanding. As you actively engage in rewriting your narrative, remember that each word you choose has the potential to shape a future of resilience, courage, and profound self-worth, for you are deserving of the love and compassion you freely offer to others.

Take Your Next Right Step

Take a moment to identify a self-limiting belief or a frequent statement your inner critic tells you that has held you back, then consider the following questions.

Have you ever found yourself trapped in a cycle of self-blame, replaying your failures until you believe they define your worth? How did this impact your ability to grow and connect with others?

_____

_____

_____

Do you relate to the constant pursuit of perfection, where external validations and societal standards seem to dictate your sense of worth?

_____

_____

_____

Do you relate to telling yourself outside success doesn't matter and you don't care anyway?

_____

_____

_____

How has that affected your self-worth and external abilities?

_____

_____

_____

Have you experienced the struggle of silencing your inner critic and embracing self-compassion? What has helped you learn to let go of regret from the past and anxiety about the future in order to find worthiness in the present moment?

_____

_____

_____

Owning Your Role

For much of my life, I clung to the role of victim, weaving a tangled web of excuses for why I stayed stuck but expected different outcomes for my repetitive actions. Blaming external factors—everything from a challenging past to contemporary societal barriers—became my shield against taking personal responsibility for this state. I would use every painful situation in my history as an excuse not to show up to learn something new or meet someone new. The fear of being "seen" kept me paralyzed from taking any action. It took a series of life-changing events for me to realize that finding true happiness rested squarely on my shoulders.

As I shared, my childhood was fraught with traumatic events, which led to tenuous relationships with my parents, especially during my teen years and into adulthood. For my own self-care, I had periods of no contact with them. For many years, I lacked the language or tools to do anything besides distance myself. Despite attempts to set aside differences, we often ended up in the same difficult place.

When my life completely unraveled, my parents were the only safety net I could rely on. They stepped up to support me, providing space and grace to heal. Their support was invaluable, though it came with its own unique challenges that didn't resolve many past hurts. Through committed trauma therapy, I gained a new understanding, recognizing that most of us aim to do our best, even if it sometimes isn't enough.

Getting Real With Yourself

At 40, it wasn't appropriate to blame them for my life's shortcomings. It became my responsibility to nurture the child inside me with the support he always needed. This realization was the first step in owning my role. The acknowledgment of your part is necessary to reconcile your past on the path to healing yourself.

Have you ever found yourself denying accountability for life's challenges?

A victim mentality is a common refuge that can obscure our ability to enact change. My wake-up call came when my world collapsed, forcing me to confront the consequences of my actions. Acknowledging my own accountability, as well as recognizing the interplay of external factors and internal patterns rooted in my history, helped me get unstuck.

When we stop making excuses and actively embrace change, we can reshape our lives on our own terms. The shift from victim to victor begins when we ask ourselves how we can learn and grow from our experiences and take ownership of our responses. Empowering language will transform your reality, so infuse your inner dialogue with encouragement. You already possess everything you need to transition from victim to leader.

This is a challenging task, and I want to emphasize that it can feel slow as you take the small steps toward change. It is not easy work, but you are worth the effort. Through continuous effort and introspection, you can reach a point where you can identify instances where you thought like a victim and then use that awareness to recognize opportunities for personal growth. Many times, I envisioned a different life for myself. Yet, whenever I faced the staircase needed to achieve change, I often stayed stuck at the bottom stair, blaming others or circumstances for why achieving that vision seemed impossible for me.

While this journey is difficult, especially for those with a resilient spirit, integrating it as a consistent, daily practice tends to make big life decisions seem more manageable. Admittedly, I am still a work in progress, but I can now forgive myself more quickly when I slip back into old patterns.

Learning to separate legitimate excuses from those we use as crutches is essential in breaking free from the cycle of victimhood. Excuses often serve as convenient justifications for avoiding uncomfortable or difficult tasks. They allow us to remain stagnant in our comfort zones rather than confronting challenges head-on. It's crucial to pause and reflect on whether these excuses are genuinely valid reasons or merely barriers constructed from our own fears and insecurities.

Own Your Role

In my journey of self-discovery, I've often used excuses to avoid facing challenges or pursuing my goals. This was especially true in my professional life. When I began re-entering the workforce, I initially sought volunteer roles, convinced that my history made me unemployable. I somehow believed that not being able to immediately step back into a high-income role meant I lacked the value to contribute meaningfully. When earning money became a necessity, I unconsciously chose to be underemployed, using work as a way to hide while healing from my past. Despite knowing I was capable of more, I spent years on the sidelines, doing just enough to get by.

However, by integrating deeper self-awareness and holding myself accountable, I've learned to distinguish between legitimate barriers and self-imposed limitations. Surrounding myself with supportive individuals who offer constructive feedback rather than criticism has been instrumental in this process. Their insights have helped me challenge my excuses and push beyond my comfort zone, ultimately facilitating personal growth and empowerment.

Reflect on areas in your life where you have felt victimized, whether in a challenging relationship, a difficult friendship, or perhaps even during your childhood. Can you trace these feelings back to formative events? Are there disempowering narratives that you tell yourself to reinforce feelings of inadequacy or your perceived inability to change circumstances? Consciously reframing these narratives and taking ownership of your role in shaping your experiences can empower you to move forward with greater agency and resilience.

As you navigate your own path, remember to question the validity of your excuses and be honest with yourself about whether they serve as genuine obstacles or convenient shields against discomfort. Seek feedback from trusted individuals who can offer constructive insights and support your journey toward breaking free from the cycle of victimhood. By embracing accountability and choosing action over excuses, you empower yourself to take control of your life and pursue your dreams with courage and determination.

Take Your Next Right Step

Reflect on accountability. In what ways have you found yourself trapped in a victim mentality? Have you made excuses or denied accountability when faced with challenging or disappointing situations?

_____

_____

_____

_____

_____

_____

_____

Create patterns of empowerment. In times of adversity, do you tend to focus more on external forces and circumstances, or do you seek ways to shape your own life using the resources available to you? Further explain the ways in which you do either or both.

_____

_____

_____

_____

_____

_____

_____

Additional Action

Step One: Identify one or two areas of your life in which you've recently noticed yourself making excuses or blaming external factors for your setbacks. Write down the most common ones you use.

_____

_____

_____

_____

Step Two: Reframe each excuse into a commitment to your own responsibility.

Examples:

Excuse: I can't find a new job because I don't have the right experience.

Reframe: I will proactively seek entry-level positions and gain experience. I'll ask others for advice on how to improve my resume.

Excuse: I'm too shy and introverted to make new friends.

Reframe: I will challenge myself to initiate conversations and invite acquaintances to meet. My personality does not limit my ability to connect.

_____

_____

_____

_____

The goal is to counter your limiting excuses with empowering statements that help you create positivity and assume accountability. Make this a regular practice in order to recognize and then dispute your most common self-sabotaging thoughts. Gain practice by doing this exercise once a day and journal how you feel.

You have more power than you think!

Failure to Move You Forward

Life is a journey marked by highs and lows, triumphs and challenges. By leveraging failures as a catalyst for personal growth, we can emerge stronger and more resilient.

It's only natural to feel discouraged or even paralyzed when setbacks arise while navigating life's complexities. The insidious voice of self-doubt might creep in, whispering notions of inadequacy. These thoughts can become a source of profound discouragement, trapping us in a mindset that stifles our progress.

But here's a radical way to reframe it: You've survived all of your worst days so far. Take a moment to celebrate your resilience, tenacity, and all of the other abilities that have seen you through to this point. Just by reading this book, you've already taken a proactive step toward building the life you desire.

The corrosive nature of self-doubt tries to convince us that our dreams are unattainable. However, we have the capacity to overcome challenges and recognize our own strengths. This is essential when shifting from a mindset of self-criticism to one of self-empowerment.

A lack of empowering perspectives or a perceived absence of support can both be formidable barriers. The beautiful truth is you can empower yourself and build a support system that is tailored to your needs. These are the choices that expand exponentially as you take the next right step. By clarifying your goals and objectives, you can create a responsive and sustaining support network to guide you through life's ups and downs.

At my lowest point, darkness enveloped everything. Waking up felt like an insurmountable task, and thoughts of giving up haunted me daily. With just a glimmer of hope, I pushed myself to take even the smallest steps forward. Some days, getting out of bed and doing basic tasks like brushing my teeth felt like major accomplishments. Setting small goals became my lifeline; each little victory fueled my determination to keep moving forward. I started with simple daily walks, which eventually became a ritual that saved me. Looking back, those walks and the quiet moments I spent in the bath were what brought me through. It was learning to reach out for support and taking those small steps every day that helped me find my way back to the light.

Failure is an effective teacher and inevitable when it comes to personal development.

But here's how you can embrace it as an opportunity to learn and grow.

- **Embrace curiosity and reflection.** Avoid tunnel vision by exploring alternative paths or solutions. Seek guidance from multiple sources and consider that there might be a smarter, more efficient way forward than one you've used in the past.
- **Learn from challenges.** Move beyond placing blame and learn from setbacks. Whether it's a failed relationship or a professional conflict, recognize your role, honor the lessons to be learned, and use it all as your stepping stones toward personal evolution.
- **Value progress over perfection.** The notion of perfection is a mirage that can hinder progress. Celebrate your achievements, no matter how small, and use them as building blocks for the future. Progress is real and sustainable.

Failures reveal what truly matters by forcing us to reconnect with our passions and values. By understanding the lessons they have to offer, we can step more fully into the life we desire. They can illuminate the gaps in our skills and highlight areas for improvement, guiding us toward a more evolved sense of self and drawing us closer to the future we envision for ourselves.

Robert Plutchik, a professor at the University of South Florida, believed humans can experience more than 34,000 unique emotions. However, most of us experience only eight primary emotions: anger, fear, sadness, joy, disgust, surprise, trust, and anticipation.

Plutchik's Wheel of Emotions helps us to understand our complex emotions, visualize the different intensities of each emotion, and gain a better understanding of the emotions created by a combination of different feelings.

To access Plutchik's Wheel of Emotions

It's crucial to not only understand what we feel but also be able to name it. Once we comprehend and distinguish our emotions from one another, we're in a better position to examine their causes. We can then develop a plan of action to avoid situations that lead to negative emotions and to immerse ourselves in environments that foster positive feelings. Understanding our emotions also allows us to be more empathetic with ourselves and others, especially when experiencing negative emotions. Knowing the root cause of these feelings helps us navigate them more effectively.

The challenge arises when people struggle to understand what they are feeling. Many tend to suppress or ignore their emotions, particularly negative ones like shame, fear, sadness, anger, or resentment. However, doing so can lead to more problems than solutions. Since there are so many different emotions, it can be challenging for people to pinpoint exactly what they are experiencing. This is where the emotion wheel comes into play—it simplifies the process of describing our emotions.

By utilizing the emotion wheel, we empower ourselves to better understand and articulate our feelings. This understanding allows us to unravel the complexities of our emotional landscape, leading to a deeper understanding of ourselves and what triggers our negative emotions. Armed with this knowledge, we can make more informed choices about how to navigate our emotional responses. Rather than succumbing to demotivating emotions like anger, sadness, or frustration, we can harness their power and use it to our advantage.

- Anger fuels our determination and inspires action.
- Sadness strengthens a sense of empathy and the connection you have with yourself.
- Frustration realigns you with your goals and could signal the need for a change in approach or environment.

These emotions are not to be feared or suppressed. Instead, they are valuable tools that can guide us toward personal growth and positive change.

When we experience anxiety, it can increase our ability to empathize and forge deeper connections with ourselves and those around us. Likewise, feeling disoriented can realign us with our objectives and indicate that we might need to modify our methods or surroundings. These feelings are not something to dread or stifle. Rather, they are invaluable resources that can lead us toward self-improvement and beneficial transformation.

Putting Emotions in Their Place

Anger was a constant presence in my life as a survivor of sexual abuse. I directed my rage at the perpetrator for violating my innocence and at my parents for not keeping me safe. This deep-seated anger permeated every relationship I had, becoming an impenetrable block that kept me from letting anyone get close.

One vivid memory from my twenties highlights the impact of this anger on my relationships. I was dating someone who genuinely cared for me and wanted to build a future together. Despite their patience and understanding, I found myself constantly pushing them away, unable to trust their intentions. Every time they tried to get emotionally closer, I would become defensive and distant. I couldn't dismiss the feeling that letting someone in meant opening myself up to the possibility of more hurt and betrayal. Through my actions, the relationship ultimately failed.

With some distance and reflection, I realized I had allowed my childhood experiences to become my identity. The anger and pain from my past became an excuse to keep my guard up, preventing me from forming deep emotional connections. I told myself that staying distant was a way to protect myself, but in reality, it was a way to avoid confronting the profound hurt and vulnerability I felt.

In therapy, I began to unpack these feelings. I recognized that my anger, while justified, was also a way to avoid the painful process of healing. It was easier to blame the perpetrator and my parents than to face the complex emotions that came with my trauma. Through intensive work, I started to understand that my anger was a barrier to the love and connection I deeply desired.

This process was incredibly challenging, but slowly, I began to dismantle the walls I had built around my heart. I learned to process my anger in healthier ways and to separate my identity from my past experiences. By doing so, I opened myself up to the possibility of genuine emotional closeness and allowed myself to experience love without the constant fear of being hurt.

My story is one of ongoing healing and growth. I still have moments of anger and fear, but I no longer let them define me or my relationships. I am learning to trust, to be vulnerable, and to let others in. Through this process,

I am reclaiming my power and creating the loving connections I once thought were impossible. Embracing these emotions as signals rather than burdens allowed me to navigate toward personal growth and positive transformations in my relationships and self-perception.

By changing my perspective and viewing failure not as a stumbling block but as a catalyst for transformation, I tapped into an immense reservoir of resilience and wisdom that exists in us all if we look for it. The key isn't to avoid setbacks but to wield them as tools to trigger my metamorphosis. Power isn't forcibly taken from us; with every finger pointed outward, we make conscious or unconscious choices to give it up.

Examining the intricate patterns of my life, I realized that perpetual reliance on others for fulfillment had actually left me unfulfilled, and then used that revelation like a compass guiding me toward empowerment. Growing from anger to self-awareness also lit the path to personal liberation. It wasn't about dismissing pain or challenges; it was about reclaiming control over my responses. No longer trapped by blame, I unearthed a wellspring of resilience within.

Recognizing that my choices, both good and bad, held the power to shape my narrative helped me recognize the uselessness of seeking outside validation. I ceased the futile search for external sources to blame when things didn't go my way. I dismantled the barriers that kept me imprisoned in cycles of anger and rose from the ashes. Strength emerges not from blaming the world for our problems but from taking responsibility for our choices. Taking action to move from anger to empowerment is about recognizing the power we possess and wielding it with intention.

How has allowing a specific emotion, such as anger, fear, or sadness, to guide your actions and decisions impacted your relationships and personal growth? Consider both the positive and negative effects, and reflect on how you might transform this guiding force into a catalyst for positive change.

_____

_____

_____

_____

_____

Turning Setbacks Into Stepping Stones

In our journey towards personal growth and empowerment, setbacks can serve as unexpected teachers, offering profound lessons that shape our resilience and perspective. One pivotal example stands out: a major career setback that initially left me feeling defeated and uncertain. I had taken on the role of interim Executive Director at a non-profit, where I had served as the board Vice President. I stepped into the role with enthusiasm and an eye on progress and growth. However, I was met with hostility from long-time staff and volunteers who were resistant to a healthier path forward. Their deliberate, malicious efforts to undermine my every move left my self-esteem in tatters and triggered deep-seated feelings of unworthiness.

Their resistance to change eventually led to a coup that ousted both the board and me as Executive Director. At the time, this felt deeply personal. However, once I stepped away, I gained a new perspective that revealed how we can become collateral damage in the crossfire of others' agendas. The odds were stacked against me from the beginning. The organization was deeply entrenched in its old ways, and change was seen as frightening and uncertain. I symbolized that fear of the unknown, making me the unintended victim of their resistance to change.

Though incredibly painful, I took some time to reflect on how I perceived the situation and the energy I was going to continue giving it. Instead of fully decompensating in despair, I eventually chose to see it as an opportunity for learning and growth. This shift in mindset allowed me to reassess my goals, develop additional skills, and ultimately steer myself toward a more fulfilling career path. I encourage you to pause and reflect on how you perceive and respond to the challenges in your own life.

Step One: Embrace Your Setbacks

Identify recent instances where setbacks, mistakes, or failures have occurred in your life. These could span personal, professional, or health-related spheres. Take a moment to jot down these examples, recognizing them as part of your unique journey. (Example: Prioritizing my health and well-being can still be a challenge. While taking steps, I still struggle to make good choices consistently.)

_____

_____

_____

_____

_____

_____

Step Two: Challenge Your Inner Critic

Next, confront the self-critical thoughts that typically arise in response to these setbacks. These thoughts might include familiar refrains like *I'm not good enough, I always mess up,* or *I'll never succeed.* Acknowledge these thoughts without judgment and write them down.

_____

_____

_____

Step Three: Rewrite with Compassion

Now, transform your self-critical statements into gentler, more compassionate reflections.

_____

_____

_____

Consider the following examples:
- **Self-Critical Statement.** I am always messing things up at work. I'll never be successful.
- **Compassionate Reflection.** I am learning and growing with each experience at work. Every mistake is an opportunity to improve and become more successful.
- **Self-Critical Statement:** I am a terrible parent. I always feel like I'm failing my kids.

- **Compassionate Reflection:** I am doing my best as a parent, and I am committed to learning and growing. My love and dedication to my kids show my true strength.

What has this setback taught me about myself or the situation?

_____

_____

_____

How can I adjust my mindset to approach similar challenges in the future?

_____

_____

_____

What aspects of this experience align with my values and goals?

_____

_____

_____

Remind yourself that you are more than this singular moment. Using compassionate reflections instead of self-critical statements is essential for fostering a healthy mindset and overall well-being. Compassionate reflections help cultivate a positive self-image and build resilience by focusing on growth and progress rather than perceived failures.

They encourage self-acceptance and reduce the harmful effects of negative self-talk, which can lead to stress, anxiety, and low self-esteem. By reframing our thoughts with kindness and understanding, we empower ourselves to learn from our mistakes and approach challenges with confidence and optimism. This shift in perspective not only enhances our mental and emotional health but also improves our relationships and overall quality of life.

Step Four: Find Meaning and Growth

Reflect on the lessons, insights, or unexpected opportunities that have emerged from each setback. Explore how reframing your perspective into positive feedback can propel you forward. Embrace the idea that every setback carries within it the seeds of growth and transformation.

The goal of this reflective exercise is not only to replace self-judgment with self-compassion but also to uncover meaningful insights from even the most challenging experiences. By practicing this approach, you nurture resilience, deepen self-awareness, and foster a mindset that embraces setbacks as crucial steps on the path to personal and professional fulfillment.

Take these steps with openness and curiosity, allowing yourself the space to grow and evolve. Embrace resilience as a guiding principle, knowing that each setback is an opportunity to discover new strengths and perspectives. Through this journey of introspection and empowerment, you lay the foundation for a more resilient and purposeful life.

Using Pain In Purpose

Pain has a transformative power in that our most challenging experiences can help guide us toward our life's purpose. Throughout this book, I've shared my journey of finding meaning in the midst of adversity and how, through thoughtful reflection, I discovered pain could be the gateway to better understanding ourselves and our mission in life. But before we look into this journey, it's crucial to acknowledge a fundamental truth: The things we do not heal continue to live inside us.

Unhealed wounds are not just memories of the past; they are the stories we bury deep within to keep ourselves safe. By pushing them down, we think we can protect ourselves from further harm. However, these hidden stories don't disappear. Instead, they manifest in various aspects of our lives—through our behaviors, our emotions, and even our physical health. The pain we try to ignore seeps into our relationships, our decision-making, and our sense of self-worth, often without us realizing it.

In my own life, I've seen how these buried stories can shape our present and future. The anger I felt as a survivor of sexual abuse, directed at both the perpetrator and my parents for not keeping me safe, became a block in every relationship. This anger prevented emotional closeness, especially with romantic partners, and kept me trapped in a cycle of pain and frustration. I tried to make sweeping changes all at once or relied on short bursts of motivation, only to find myself back at square one when old habits resurfaced.

It was only when I started to show up consistently, even on days when I didn't feel particularly motivated, that real progress began to unfold.

Life's challenges, which may seem insurmountable, can actually catalyze personal growth by revealing our hidden strengths. During our darkest moments, we discover resilience and untapped potential, empowering us to move forward with renewed vigor. It's crucial to regularly reflect on the strengths we uncover through adversity. This process transforms us into individuals of unyielding strength.

> *Pain has the extraordinary ability to deepen our sense of empathy and compassion—for ourselves and others.*

By confronting our struggles and enduring the pain they bring, we also develop a profound understanding of the human experience. The depth of emotion that follows allows us to authentically support others on their journey and foster genuine connections.

Every hardship can help clarify our values and priorities. It's important to ask ourselves: How has this hardship clarified what matters most to me? By identifying our core values through painful experiences, we gain a clearer vision of our life's purpose. With this clarity, we can navigate the world with intention, purpose, and authenticity.

Difficult times are not roadblocks; they are stepping stones. They are not permanent obstacles but temporary challenges that can transform into opportunities if we choose to see them differently.

But the journey to find meaning in pain is not without its challenges. Unprocessed emotions and the fear of scrutiny can hinder our progress. It's essential to acknowledge these hurdles as we encounter them and take deliberate steps to properly process our emotions.

It can be challenging to find meaning in painful experiences when one hasn't fully processed the aftermath. It's crucial to acknowledge the pain, explore it, and ask thoughtful questions that guide and shape how you think about the scenario and apply it to others in the future. Some experiences may be too difficult to reexamine right away, but acknowledging your capacity to look at them in a new light at some point later on, can lead to profound insights and propel you forward in unexpected ways.

While personal reflection can be difficult and time-consuming, it is a powerful tool. Through self-care practices like journaling, we can process our emotions, reframe our mindsets, and extract critical lessons from challenging periods in our lives. Finding my purpose has been a convoluted and lengthy process. Journaling has been crucial, offering me a space to process my emotions without judgment or shame. My journal evolved into a personal manifesto where I could openly explore and reveal parts of myself.

For example, during my time as interim Executive Director of a non-profit, I was painfully made an example of because of others' agendas. My value was overlooked, and decisions were made based on their priorities, not my contributions. Journaling became instrumental in helping me navigate this turmoil and uncover hidden passions. Instead of completely succumbing to despair, I used journaling to view the situation as a chance for learning and growth. This shift in mindset allowed me to reassess my goals, develop new skills, and ultimately chart a course toward a more fulfilling career path aligned with my values and aspirations.

As you read, I invite you to reflect on your own journey. Consider the stories you have buried and the pain you have yet to heal. Know that these experiences hold the key to a deeper understanding of yourself and your mission in life. Embrace the shadows, for within them lies the potential for profound transformation. Together, let us embark on this journey of healing and self-discovery, unlocking the true power of our pain and uncovering the purpose that lies within.

Take Your Next Right Step

What unhealed wounds from your past continue to influence your present behaviors, emotions, and relationships? Reflect on the stories you have buried and consider how they might be manifesting in your daily life.

_____

_____

_____

_____

During your darkest moments, what hidden strengths and resilience have you discovered within yourself? Think about how you have navigated challenges and what personal growth emerged from those experiences.

_____

_____

_____

_____

How have your hardships clarified your values and priorities? Ask yourself, *How did this hardship clarify what matters most to me?* Explore how these realizations have shaped your path.

_____

_____

_____

_____

_____

What practices, such as journaling or meditation, have helped you process your emotions and find meaning in difficult experiences? Reflect on the tools and methods you have used to navigate through pain and how they have contributed to your personal growth.

_____

_____

_____

_____

_____

PART III
Taking Steps to Support Yourself

Progressing to Growth and Fulfillment

In the pursuit of personal and professional growth, focusing on progress transcends the constraints of striving for perfection. This shift encourages us to not expect flawless execution in every aspect of our lives but to commit to the journey and appreciate the cumulative impact of our growth. All too often, we get lost in thinking that someone else is able to do something smarter, faster, or better. These fears are rarely grounded in truth and often serve consistently taking the next right step.

Perfection Isn't Real

Perfectionism, with its unattainable standards, stifles us and hinders our ability to embrace opportunities for growth and change as an internal stalling tactic. By constantly comparing ourselves to others and imagining we fall short, we create a mental barrier that prevents us from taking risks and pursuing our passions. This mindset can paralyze us, making us hesitant to start new projects or take on challenges that could lead to significant personal and professional development.

Focusing on progress allows us to shed this burden and navigate life with purpose and resilience. Welcoming a progress-oriented mindset means valuing each step forward, no matter how small, and recognizing that imperfection is a natural and essential part of the learning process. It shifts our focus from a fear of failure to an appreciation of growth, enabling us to take bold steps, make mistakes, and learn from them without the crushing weight of unrealistic expectations.

The Power of Progress

By valuing progress, we open ourselves to a world of possibilities where growth becomes the goal rather than an elusive state of perfection. This approach fosters a growth mindset, viewing challenges as opportunities to develop our skills and expand our horizons. It encourages self-compassion, acknowledging that everyone has their own unique journey and pace. Embracing progress allows us to build resilience and adaptability, helping us navigate life's complexities with grace and determination. Ultimately, this shift empowers us to live more fulfilling lives, pursuing our dreams and aspirations without the paralyzing fear of not measuring up to an impossible ideal.

At the heart of this concept lies the understanding that significant change is not always born from grandiose leaps but rather from the accumulation of small, deliberate actions over time. Each step, no matter how modest, contributes to our overall trajectory. It is the commitment and consistency applied to these incremental steps that hold the power to create lasting, meaningful transformation.

Consider the image of a sculptor crafting a masterpiece. The chisel strikes the stone repeatedly, each tap contributing to the final form. Similarly, when we focus our daily efforts on progress, we chip away at the barriers that impede our growth and reveal our true potential.

Welcoming Progress

Celebrating small victories triggers the release of dopamine—the brain's reward neurotransmitter—and reinforces positive behavior, motivating continued effort. Focusing on progress initiates a positive feedback loop that propels us forward on our journey of self-improvement.

I encourage you to welcome the freedom that comes with focusing on progress rather than achieving perfection. Doing so provides evidence-based insight to empower you as you embark on a journey where every small step is acknowledged as a victory, and the pursuit of progress becomes a sustainable, fulfilling path.

Start Where You Are

The next right step begins with recognizing your current state and what you can do immediately rather than focusing on what you want to do later. Simple actions like journaling, walking, reconnecting with friends, and actively practicing gratitude all qualify as meaningful steps.

Additionally, discern the value of having an accountability partner who can support and motivate you. Whether it's a trusted friend, mentor, or coach, an accountability partner can provide encouragement and honest feedback to keep you on track. For the goals you choose to keep to yourself, maintaining personal commitment and consistently taking steps forward is crucial. Balancing both public accountability and personal responsibility will help you stay motivated and focused on your journey.

Small steps help build momentum over time. Whether it's writing three things you're grateful for daily, taking a short walk, or maintaining healthy sleep habits, choose steps that align with your values and goals.

Courage When You Feel Completely Stuck

When you feel completely stuck, identify the smallest step you can take. For instance, someone battling depression might start their healing journey by completing simple tasks like unloading the dishwasher or cleaning one side of the kitchen counter. Every step matters.

Consistency is more important than the size of the steps you take. Commit to your chosen actions, trusting that over time, they will become habits. Small steps, when combined with your existing routine, create a compounding effect that leads to significant change.

The "next right step" concept is designed to break you free from stagnation. It starts with the present moment and acknowledges that you don't have to climb the whole staircase at once. Adopt the idea that progress, not perfection, is key, and focus on taking small, manageable steps that align with your values. Every modest but determined step you take today is a gift your future self will appreciate.

Take Your Next Right Step

What is one small step you can take today that aligns with your goals and values? Identify a manageable action that you can confidently commit to and take that step forward.

_____

_____

_____

_____

_____

_____

_____

_____

How can you celebrate your progress, no matter how small, to stay motivated and focused on your journey? Find ways to acknowledge and celebrate your achievements, reinforcing the positive impact of your efforts.

_____

_____

_____

_____

_____

_____

_____

What practices or tools can you incorporate into your daily routine to help you stay mindful and intentional about taking the next right step? Explore methods such as journaling, meditation, or setting daily intentions to maintain focus and clarity.

_____

_____

_____

_____

_____

_____

Claiming Your Worth With Self-Care

This chapter highlights the importance of showing up for yourself daily—an art steeped in consistency, self-love, and acknowledging your intrinsic value. I discovered numerous insights from dipping my toes into countless self-help techniques, trying everything from vision boards and affirmations to radical goal-setting. Despite all these tools, I struggled to turn inspiration into sustainable change. Old habits eventually reclaimed their place in my routine while my journal gathered dust.

You deserve to have someone in your corner, and that person is you!

Change Comes Through Small, Consistent Actions

I've come to realize the path to lasting positive change is a marathon, not a sprint. It's rooted in authenticity and small, consistent actions, as well as committing to behaviors that align with your innermost values. It's about understanding that sustainable change comes through daily, intentional practices, not sudden leaps. Let's shift our focus to incremental progress rather than instant results. Like a marathon runner, it's crucial to understand that momentum builds gradually and to pace ourselves. I spent decades seeking shortcuts without realizing that lasting transformation is achieved through renewing intentions and steadfast devotion to showing up for myself every day.

Use Reflection as Your Guide

When stress or turbulence makes our world feel stormy, reflection can help us extract valuable lessons from both calm and challenging times. Engaging in reflective practices, like journaling, meditation, and mindful walks, gently attends to our hearts and prepares us for new insights. These rituals highlight that self-care should be an integral part of our lives, not just a checklist item.

During stressful periods, it's easy to feel overwhelmed and lose our sense of direction. By stepping back in reflection, we gain clarity and perspective. These practices offer a safe space to process emotions and experiences without judgment, fostering a deeper connection with ourselves. Regularly engaging in these routines helps build self-awareness, which is especially valuable during turbulent times.

Commit to A Daily Practice

At center stage is the concept of commitment, which we might consider as a nuanced scale ranging from one to ten. This intentional approach underscores the necessity of choosing actions with a higher commitment level. Imagine waking up to perform sacred morning rituals that ground you in gratitude and set the tone for days filled with intention that is aligned with your life's purpose. These rituals, from meditation to movement, become the threads weaving wholeness into the fabric of your every day. Pick those actions that you can commit to at a level eight, nine, or ten. Doing so will make sustainability more likely.

Integrating careful and thoughtful criteria that aligns with your personal goals and values fosters genuine commitment. In other words, if your next step doesn't command a high level of commitment, it's not your next right step. The key lies in establishing consistent rituals that serve your needs and can easily become second nature. These habits accumulate over time, leading to wholehearted shifts in your life for the better. This is a gentle reminder to seek progress over perfection.

Build Sustainable Routines

Establishing healthy patterns requires repeating positive habits. Be patient but persistent. Over time, these conscious choices will transform your life because prioritizing yourself fuels the self-love and empowerment required to get unstuck. Remember, you deserve to have someone in your corner, and that person is you! Each step you take solidifies your value of commitment and consistency in achieving lasting change.

In the past, I fell into the trap of trying to make sweeping changes all at once or relying on short bursts of motivation. I would set ambitious goals, only to find that old habits would quickly resurface, leading to setbacks. Real progress began when I integrated the strategy of showing up consistently, even on days when I didn't feel particularly motivated. This shift in approach allowed me to build lasting habits and make steady progress over time.

You can build sustainable routines that support growth but don't rely on motivation alone. Make promises to your future self, and then keep them. Set reminders that help reinforce new, positive habits. Celebrate small wins and readjust your expectations after your missteps. Understand that change is a marathon, not a sprint, and that consistency builds over time. Be patient with yourself and stay focused on progress because commitment means choosing your path again every day and living for your future self.

Incorporate Self-Care Rituals

Make sacred space for self-care in some way, then start showing up for yourself every day. There's no need for grand gestures when small, intentional actions compound over time into the profound gift of self-acceptance and inner peace. For example, a friend created a small space in her closet where she kept a candle, crystals, and her "One Day at a Time" book. Her kids couldn't find her there, and she would set a timer for a quick meditation. This dedicated space became a sanctuary, allowing her to consistently nurture her well-being. In the journey toward recognizing your inherent worth, you have to take that first step. It's a testament to the beautiful symphony of your own existence. Show up, commit, and let the journey paint your life with the hues of self-love and authenticity.

Center Yourself in Stillness

In exploring ways to center yourself in stillness, meditation is a powerful self-care practice that fosters mental clarity and emotional stability. However, if meditation doesn't appeal to you, there are other ways to achieve stillness and reflection, such as a gentle walk, quiet reflection time, or journaling. By creating a space for stillness and reflection, meditation allows you to disconnect from daily stressors and connect with your inner self. This practice encourages mindfulness, helping to reduce anxiety, enhance concentration, and promote a sense of inner peace. Through regular meditation, you can cultivate resilience, better manage stress, and develop a more profound understanding of your thoughts and emotions, ultimately leading to a more balanced and fulfilling life. Here are a few tips to ease into meditation for those who've been hesitant or disinterested:

- **Start small.** Begin with just a few minutes each day. Set a timer for 5 minutes and focus on your breath or a simple affirmation that validates your intended outcome. Gradually increase the duration as you become more comfortable.

- **Find your rhythm.** Experiment with different times of day to meditate and see what works best for you. Some people find that meditating first thing in the morning helps set a positive tone for the day, while others prefer to unwind with meditation in the evening before bed.
- **Embrace guided meditation.** If the idea of sitting in silence feels daunting, try guided meditation apps or videos. These provide gentle prompts and instructions to help keep your mind focused and ease you into the practice.
- **Be gentle with yourself.** It's natural for thoughts to wander during meditation, especially when you're just starting out. Instead of getting frustrated or discouraged, simply acknowledge the thought and gently guide your attention back to your breath or chosen focal point.

Trust Your Own Timing

Succumbing to societal pressure to produce immediate results is an unrealistic practice. Doing so dismantles the illusion of real and sustainable change and emphasizes a lack of patience and self-reflection. Life's inherent messiness rarely offers solace to those on transformative journeys who could benefit from accepting the wisdom of gradual progress. A simple gratitude mantra or taking five minutes to relish a sunset and toast the gifts in your life: self-care does not necessarily demand extensive time when done consciously. The key lies in the unwavering commitment to showing up for yourself daily.

Guard Your Vision and Value

Navigating whom to trust with your ideas and dreams can be a delicate balance. While having supportive friends is invaluable, their involvement can sometimes complicate matters. Seeking random opinions from others may only add confusion to the mix. In reality, you deserve a solid support system—a person or group that understands your vision and champions your potential, whether it's a trusted friend, mentor, or yourself. Protecting your dreams from unnecessary interference is paramount. Trust those who offer constructive feedback without imposing their own agenda. By surrounding yourself with the right people, you can create an environment where your ideas can thrive.

By embracing self-care, you claim your worth through small, consistent actions rooted in authenticity and reflection. This journey is not about grand gestures but about daily practices that align with your deepest values and goals. By establishing sustainable routines, engaging in positive reinforcement, and trusting the right support system, you create a foundation for lasting change. Prioritizing self-care rituals like meditation and journaling helps you navigate life's challenges with clarity and resilience. Remember, real transformation comes from showing up for yourself every day, celebrating progress over perfection, and committing to your well-being. You deserve to be in your own corner, championing your growth and celebrating your intrinsic worth.

Take Your Next Right Step

Step One: Commit to a morning ritual. Start your day with a grounding exercise like meditation or light movement. Choose actions that align with your life's highest purpose for that day. Ensure your choice has a commitment level of eight, nine, or ten.

_____

_____

_____

_____

_____

_____

Step Two: Take time for an evening reflection to learn from both easier and more challenging experiences. Make it a daily routine to nurture growth. Write down an intention you'd like to focus on for the next day.

_____

_____

_____

_____

Step Three: Start small, but commit big. This means integrating small but committed actions into your routine. Practice patience and self-reflection, whether through a gratitude mantra or a brief sunset reflection. What are the small actions you can take to create a snowball effect of change? Write them down.

_____

_____

_____

_____

_____

_____

Step Four: Supply your own positive reinforcement when you journal. Start a journal in which you can celebrate your small wins. Acknowledge accomplishments to help build confidence and understand that each step forward is a significant achievement. Make this fun! Buy a package of stickers, draw in the margins, or insert emojis if using an online journal.

Dialing in Your Vision

In a world brimming with noise, opinions, and distractions, finding and maintaining clarity about your vision can feel like trying to catch lightning bugs in a storm. It's easy to become overwhelmed by external expectations and to lose sight of what truly resonates with your soul. Yet, clarity of vision is crucial for living a purposeful and fulfilling life. It requires introspection, courage, and the willingness to honor your deepest desires over the dictates of others.

The Echoes of Your Soul

Each of us has an inner compass, a part of ourselves that quietly but persistently nudges us toward what we are meant to pursue. This inner guidance system often manifests as a recurring thought, an unfulfilled dream, or a passion that won't be silenced. It's what I call the "nagging whisper"—that gentle but insistent voice within you that keeps urging you towards a specific goal or vision.

Recognizing and honoring this inner whisper is vital. It's the part of you that knows what you truly want beyond the surface-level desires and the pressures of societal expectations. It's important to regularly check in with yourself to assess whether you are aligning your actions with this core vision or if you're drifting away from it.

The Trap of External Expectations

One of the biggest obstacles to achieving clarity is the influence of external expectations. Society, family, and friends often have their own ideas about what success and happiness should look like. While these perspectives can be valuable, they can also create a smokescreen that obscures your true desires.

When you start pursuing goals based on what others expect from you, you risk living a life that isn't truly yours. For example, you might find yourself in a career that you're not passionate about simply because it was deemed prestigious or financially rewarding. Or you might pursue a certain lifestyle or set of achievements to gain approval from others, rather than out of a genuine desire.

To break free from this trap, it's essential to distinguish between what you truly want and what you think you should want. This requires an honest and sometimes uncomfortable examination of your motives and values. Ask yourself:

What am I genuinely passionate about?

_____

_____

_____

What activities or goals consistently energize me?

_____

_____

_____

What would I pursue if there were no limits or expectations?

_____

_____

_____

The Courage to Be True to Yourself

Having clarity about your vision is not just about identifying what you want; it's also about having the courage to act on it. This often means stepping beyond your ego and the comfort of conforming to what's familiar or expected. It requires a deep level of self-awareness and bravery to pursue a path that might be unconventional or misunderstood by others. Courage in this context means:

- **Embracing Authenticity.** Allow yourself to be vulnerable and honest about what you truly want, even if it defies conventional norms or what others might expect from you.
- **Facing Resistance.** Understand that pursuing your true vision might come with resistance, both from within yourself and from external sources. Be prepared to face doubts and criticisms and use them as fuel to reinforce your commitment.
- **Taking Inspired Action.** Clarity of vision is not just about knowing what you want; it's also about taking concrete steps towards making it a reality. This involves setting clear goals, making plans, and consistently working towards them, even when progress seems slow.

Practical Steps to Cultivate Your Vision

- **Regular Reflection.** Set aside time for regular self-reflection. This can be done through journaling, meditation, or quiet contemplation. Use this time to explore your feelings and thoughts about your vision and how closely your current actions align with it.
- **Seek Inspiration.** Surround yourself with people, books, and experiences that inspire you. Exposure to new ideas and perspectives can help clarify your own vision and ignite your passion.
- **Test Your Vision.** Experiment with small steps or projects that align with your vision. This can provide valuable insights into whether your vision is a true reflection of your desires or if adjustments are needed.
- **Create a Vision Board.** Visual representation can be a powerful tool. Create a vision board that reflects your goals and aspirations. Place it where you can see it daily to keep your vision at the forefront of your mind.
- **Stay Flexible.** Understand that clarity is a process, not a one-time achievement. Your vision might evolve as you grow and change, and that's okay. Be open to adjusting your course as needed while staying true to your core desires.

Rewards of a Clear Vision

When you are clear about your vision and act upon it, the rewards are profound. You will find a sense of purpose and fulfillment that comes from living authentically. Your actions will be more deliberate and aligned with your true self, leading to greater satisfaction and success.

Moreover, clarity of vision helps to streamline your energy and efforts. Instead of scattering your focus across various distractions and unfulfilling pursuits, you'll direct your resources toward what genuinely matters to you.

This focused approach can lead to accelerated progress and deeper satisfaction with your achievements.

The importance of being clear on your vision cannot be overstated. It involves checking in with yourself, paying attention to the persistent whispers of your soul, and having the courage to pursue what truly resonates with you. By stepping beyond ego and external expectations and by embracing your authentic desires, you set yourself on a path to a more meaningful and fulfilling life. Cultivate your vision with intention and dedication and watch as it transforms into a powerful reality.

Discovering Your Boundaries

The significance of healthy boundaries is rooted in understanding how their absence can keep us tethered to unfulfilling patterns. The tendency to exhaust ourselves by prioritizing others' needs over our fulfillment becomes prevalent. This chapter explores the intricate ways that boundaries, or a lack thereof, can shape personal growth and fulfillment, as well as issues like toxic relationships, overcommitment, and negative self-talk.

Identify Areas That Need Boundaries

A crucial step in harnessing the power of boundaries is a thoughtful exploration of various facets of your life in which you would most benefit from their establishment. Imagine your life as a complex tapestry woven with threads of different colors and textures, each representing its most distinct aspects: physical, emotional, mental, spiritual, and temporal.

Physical boundaries are where your well-being is intricately tied to your energy and personal space. This might include recognizing when to say "no" to commitments that drain your physical resources or learning to prioritize self-care without guilt.

How do I allocate my energy and utilize my personal space?

_____

_____

_____

_____

When do I feel drained, and what activities or commitments contribute to this feeling?

_____

_____

_____

_____

How can I prioritize self-care without guilt?

_____

_____

_____

_____

For **emotional boundaries**, identify relationships that might be emotionally draining. You might then set clear expectations with friends or family members about the kind of support you can provide them without compromising your well-being.

Which relationships are emotionally draining?

_____

_____

_____

_____

What do I expect in terms of emotional support from my loved ones?

_____

_____

_____

_____

How can I communicate clear boundaries without compromising my well-being?

_____

_____

_____

_____

Evaluate the demands you place on yourself for work, family, projects, and personal goals. Establishing boundaries in these areas might mean acknowledging limitations, avoiding over-commitment, and recognizing when it's time to step back and recharge.

What demands do I place on myself for work, family, projects, or personal goals?

_____

_____

_____

When do I recognize my limits, and when do I overcommit? Is there a pattern there? (Example: I overcommit with family and undercommit at work.)

_____

_____

_____

What signs indicate that it's time for me to step back and recharge? How can I better pay attention to those signs?

_____

_____

_____

To address **spiritual boundaries**, reflect on activities or engagements that best align with your beliefs and values. This may involve setting boundaries around how you engage with spiritual practices or participate in activities that resonate with your inner self.

Which activities or engagements align most with my beliefs and values?

_____

_____

_____

How can I set boundaries around the time I spend on spiritual practices or activities?

_____

_____

_____

Temporal boundaries are intertwined with all aspects of our lives. Recognizing the limits on your time is crucial. This could mean learning to say "no" to time-consuming activities that do not contribute to your growth or well-being.

What are the limits on my time, and do they align with my priorities?

_____

_____

_____

How often do I find it challenging to say "no" to time-consuming activities or people that do not contribute to my growth or well-being? Do I recognize the "why" behind this?

_____

_____

_____

Set Boundaries With Compassion

This section guides you through a nuanced process of self-discovery and encourages you to recognize the specific threads in your life's tapestry where boundaries are needed most. Learning the delicate art of setting boundaries requires both a firm hand and compassion. It's a journey that asks you to reflect on how you express your needs and limits while also being mindful of the emotions involved—yours and those of others.

Consider the short-term discomfort that accompanies establishing boundaries. This discomfort can act as a preventive measure, shielding you from the potential long-term pain and stagnation that may arise otherwise. It's important to consider questions that prompt self-reflection and empower you to effectively express boundaries.

_____

_____

_____

_____

_____

What fears or concerns arise when you imagine setting boundaries that make you feel discomfort? How can you address this?

_____
_____
_____
_____
_____
_____

Reflect on instances in which the idea of short-term discomfort prevented you from taking on prolonged challenges. Expressing boundaries might be challenging, but you can learn to navigate it with grace.

In what ways can you refine your communication habits to make your boundaries more clear and effective?

_____
_____
_____
_____
_____
_____

Embrace the knowledge that healthy boundaries are not only an act of self-love but also a testament to self-respect. By establishing and maintaining these boundaries, you can reclaim control over your life.

Can you recall any moments when implementing boundaries positively influenced your overall well-being? Describe that situation and how you felt after.

_____

_____

_____

In what areas of your life do you envision the restoration of balance through implementing healthy boundaries?

_____

_____

_____

Overcome Resistance to Setting Boundaries

Establishing boundaries requires acknowledging and overcoming the inherent resistance that arises when we set out to do so. This means exploring the roots of resistance and unraveling complexities tied to common causes of it, such as fear, conflict avoidance, lack of self-worth, guilt, and difficulty discerning personal needs.

Through this deeper examination, you'll gain valuable insight into the intricate web of emotions and beliefs that contribute to this resistance.

What fears or thoughts frequently hold you back from setting clear boundaries?

_____

_____

_____

_____

How does avoiding conflict impact your ability to establish limits?

_____

_____

_____

_____

In what ways does your sense of self-worth influence your willingness to prioritize your needs?

_____

_____

_____

_____

Reflect on instances in which guilt has hindered your efforts to set boundaries. Acknowledge the challenges you face in discerning your needs amid the demands of daily life. Explore personalized approaches to conquer these challenges while recognizing that understanding the root of resistance is a key step toward reclaiming your agency.

How can you reframe fear as an opportunity for growth rather than an obstacle?

_____

_____

_____

_____

In what situations can you use assertiveness to overcome the tendency to avoid conflict?

_____

_____

_____

_____

Tangible methods can boost your sense of self-worth and reinforce the importance of prioritizing needs, like implementing compassionate practices you can integrate to alleviate the guilt we associate with setting boundaries.

By confronting resistance head-on, I've discovered a profound impact on my personal relationships, particularly with my partner. Addressing barriers to setting boundaries has been crucial. For instance, I used to avoid discussing sensitive topics to prevent conflicts, which led to misunderstandings and unresolved issues. Recognizing this pattern, we committed to open and honest communication, even when it felt uncomfortable. By consistently practicing this approach, we've learned to navigate conflicts constructively, deepening our understanding and trust in each other. This approach has empowered me to express myself authentically and fostered a more fulfilling and supportive relationship overall.

Healthy boundaries play a pivotal role in crafting the life you desire. By recognizing and establishing them, you can escape unfulfilling patterns and dive into every aspect of your life—physical, emotional, spiritual, and temporal—using reflective questions as your compass. These inquiries will steer you toward self-discovery.

Through committed, meaningful action, you can learn to set boundaries while acknowledging short-term discomfort as a preventive measure against long-term pain and stagnation. Personalize this journey by reflecting on your previous approaches, fears, and instances in which boundaries enhanced your well-being.

Setting Healthy Boundaries

Setting healthy boundaries is crucial for maintaining your well-being, self-esteem, and overall life satisfaction. Boundaries act as a protective measure, safeguarding your mental, emotional, and physical health from being compromised by external pressures. They enable you to prioritize your needs and values, ensuring that your energy is directed towards relationships and commitments that respect and support your personal growth. By clearly defining and communicating your limits, you create a balanced environment where mutual respect thrives. This process not only enhances your sense of self-worth but also fosters healthier, more fulfilling interactions. Implementing boundaries is an essential step toward living authentically and achieving a sustainable, empowered life.

Step One: Identify current relationships or commitments for which you neglect your needs. These might be with a family member, a friend, a boss, a co-worker, etc.

_____

_____

_____

_____

Step Two: Reflect on what healthy boundaries would look like for those relationships. What specifically do you need to communicate or implement?

Examples:
1. Limiting time spent listening without reciprocity.
2. Leaving a situation if it becomes toxic.
3. Setting firm work hours to protect personal time.
4. Saying no to tasks that overburden you.
5. Choose any others that feel aligned for you.

_____

_____

_____

Step Three: Develop scripts to clearly yet compassionately communicate these boundaries to the other parties involved. I've given you some examples with which we can close this chapter. Take your list from above and craft your own scripts, making sure to practice them in order to execute the boundary in the moment when you may be nervous.

With a Family Member
- I've been reflecting on our interactions lately, and I wanted to talk to you about something important. Some of your comments about my personal life make me uneasy and feel like an invasion of privacy.
- I value our relationship, and I believe that setting clear boundaries will help us communicate better. So, from now on, I'd like to keep certain aspects of my personal life private.
- I hope you understand that this is for my emotional well-being, and I believe it will strengthen our connection and help us respect each other's boundaries.
- Thanks for understanding.

With a Friend
- Hey there, I wanted to chat with you about something important. Lately, our late-night calls have been negatively affecting my sleep and daily routine. I really enjoy our talks, but I need to focus on my well-being.
- So, I was thinking that maybe we could try to chat earlier in the evening or find a time that works better for us both. I want us to stay connected, but I also need to take care of myself.
- Thanks for being open to this.

With a Coworker
- I'd like to address something regarding our work dynamic. I've noticed that personal conversations are taking up a significant portion of my work time, and it's starting to impact my productivity.
- To ensure I can focus on my tasks and maintain efficiency, I need to set limits on the time spent engaging in personal discussions during work hours. This will help me prioritize my core responsibilities and get my work done more effectively.
- I hope you understand that this boundary is important for maintaining my productivity. I value our teamwork and want to ensure I contribute my best.
- Thank you for understanding. Can we find a way to balance personal conversations and work tasks so that I can stay on track?

Step Four: How will setting these boundaries impact your self-esteem, energy, fulfillment, and growth? What changes do you hope to see?

_____

_____

_____

Recognize the profound value of setting healthy boundaries in your life.

Boundaries are not just about protecting yourself; they are about honoring your worth and ensuring that your relationships and commitments reflect mutual respect and understanding.

By taking action to establish and communicate clear boundaries, you empower yourself to prioritize your well-being and maintain a healthy balance in all areas of your life.

Remember, the short-term discomfort of asserting your needs is far outweighed by the long-term benefits of emotional stability, increased self-esteem, and deeper, more meaningful connections. Embrace the power of boundaries as a testament to your self-respect, and take the necessary steps today to create a life that truly honors your value.

Supporting Yourself with Consistency and Care

Establishing healthy boundaries is empowering, but maintaining them effectively requires continuous commitment and reflection. As you continue on this path, it's essential to regularly assess the boundaries you've established. Life circumstances evolve, and what once worked may need adjustment to continue effectively supporting your well-being. Reflect on any challenges you've encountered in maintaining the boundaries you set. Understanding where you struggle can help you strategize more effectively for the future.

Consistent communication is key to maintaining boundaries effectively. Regularly reinforce your boundaries with clarity and assertiveness. Address boundary violations promptly and assertively, reinforcing their importance while respecting the feelings of others.

How can you improve your communication of boundaries to ensure they are respected?

_____

_____

_____

How do you typically handle situations where your boundaries are crossed?

_____

_____

_____

Self-awareness and self-care play crucial roles in sustaining boundaries. Stay attuned to your needs and prioritize self-care activities that recharge you emotionally, physically, and mentally. Be flexible and adaptable in your approach to boundaries. As circumstances change, be willing to adjust your boundaries accordingly.

How do you currently prioritize self-care in your daily life, and what adjustments can you make to ensure it aligns with your boundary maintenance?

_____

_____

_____

How comfortable are you with adapting your boundaries to changing situations, and what strategies can you implement to navigate these changes effectively?

_____

_____

_____

Seeking support is another essential aspect of boundary maintenance. Lean on your support network for guidance and encouragement when facing challenges with boundaries.

Who in your life can you turn to for support in maintaining healthy boundaries?

_____

_____

_____

If you are struggling to set and maintain boundaries, you may consider professional support, like therapy, counseling, or coaching, to explore deeper issues related to boundary setting and maintenance. Recognize that maintaining boundaries may present feelings of guilt, fear of conflict, or pushback from others.

How do these challenges manifest in your life, and what steps can you take to address them more effectively?

_____

_____

_____

Maintaining boundaries is a dynamic process that requires ongoing attention and effort. By staying mindful of your needs, communicating effectively, practicing self-care, and seeking support, you empower yourself to sustain boundaries that promote your well-being and personal growth. Celebrate your successes along the way, noting how maintaining boundaries has positively impacted your relationships and self-esteem. Reflect on recent successes to acknowledge your boundary-setting journey and how you can build upon these achievements to move forward.

PART IV

Living Empowered and Unstuck

Making Gratitude a Daily Practice

The profound impact that cultivating gratitude can have serves as a cornerstone for sustainable change. In the intricate maze of life, gratitude leads us to find silver linings and guides us along the expansive journey of personal growth.

Gratitude, especially when faced with challenges, cuts through the fog that obscures blessings and positive experiences. Life's major hurdles naturally draw our focus to our problems, especially in the midst of trauma or adversity. The ability to truly feel grateful necessitates a shift in mindset from discouragement and frustration to acknowledgment and appreciation for the beauty within life's complexities.

Practicing gratitude unveils the goodness that is woven through our existence. Consistent methods like keeping a journal or connecting with your higher power are essential tools for redirecting one's focus while staying encouraged during difficult seasons. A journal, when used daily, offers comfort and perspective during times when it might be difficult to pinpoint our blessings. The mind can be trained to spot positives, countering the deeply ingrained negativity bias that clouds our perceptions. As with anything, this takes practice to maintain.

The positive impact of cultivating gratitude in our physical, emotional, and mental well-being is profound and far-reaching. Beyond its role in improving emotional resilience and enhancing mental health processes, which can be likened to the benefits of meditation, gratitude also contributes to reduced inflammation, improved heart health, deeper personal connections, and an overall sense of satisfaction and happiness.

Integrating gratitude into our daily routines is a vital aspect of the transformative journey we've discussed in this book. Whether through journaling, sharing aloud during family dinners, or silently reflecting during spiritual practices, the key lies in letting gratitude arise naturally. Whatever you choose to incorporate into your routine, tailor the method to your unique style and ensure that the practice remains sincere, authentic, and consistent.

Focusing on what you are thankful for makes the process of growth and change more seamless, and gratitude engenders optimism and motivation to tackle challenges.

Offering regular pep talks to your future self nurtures a mindset of abundance rather than scarcity and shifts the perception of growth so that it no longer looks like arduous work but a harmonious and naturally unfolding cycle.

For those struggling with finding gratitude on tougher days, gentle advice should prevail. Be kind to yourself and avoid unnecessary pressure to achieve perfection. Recall previous chapters where we learned how to focus on small wins and share our struggles with a trusted support system. Trust in the resilience of your spirit, knowing that gratitude will come when the storm passes.

Embrace the power of gratitude. Let it be your guiding light, a steadfast companion on your journey, and a wellspring of strength that propels you forward with appreciation, positivity, and profound change. There is a power in gratitude that is unmatched.

Take Your Next Right Step

Commit to recognizing gratitude in your journal on a daily basis to help reframe your mindset and encourage positive momentum during this journey of transformation. Each morning or evening, find a quiet space to reflect on whatever you feel genuinely grateful for (ideally, you pick at least three things). These can be big or small: a sunny day, a positive chat with a friend, achieving a goal at work, etc.

_____

_____

_____

_____

Write down each item and a couple of sentences on why it matters to you or how it impacted you positively. If the same items come up repeatedly, challenge yourself to notice new things.

_____

_____

_____

_____

Set a five-minute timer and journal honestly, even if some days feel like they've yielded more abundance than others. Consistency is what matters most in this practice. Keep your entries together in a gratitude journal or reflection app. When you face setbacks or discouragement, reread previous posts to rediscover hope and all the silver linings hiding in plain sight. What changed for you as thankfulness became part of your daily rhythm? Stick with this practice for the next thirty days, tracking any shifts in your overall mindset, resiliency, and well-being.

_____

_____

_____

_____

_____

Living in the Present Moment

Imagine waking up one morning and realizing that the entire day ahead of you is a blank canvas, an opportunity to shape and mold into whatever you desire. Now, imagine you're so preoccupied with regrets about yesterday's missed chances and anxieties about tomorrow's uncertainties that you completely overlook the masterpiece you could create with the hours right in front of you. It sounds like a tragic waste, doesn't it? Yet, this is the everyday reality for many of us. We're often trapped in the past or consumed by the future, losing sight of the only time we truly have: the present moment.

The Elusive Now

We've all heard the phrase "live in the moment," but understanding and applying this concept in our lives can be challenging. We live in a world that constantly bombards us with information and distractions, which can make staying grounded in the present feel like an almost impossible task. It's so easy to get caught up in what has happened or what might happen, but what about what is happening right now?

The present moment is where all our power lies. It's where action happens and where change can be made. The past is behind us, a series of events that we cannot alter no matter how much we wish to. The future, while it holds potential, is still a realm of possibilities that we can't control until it becomes the present. The only time we can influence is now.

Traps of the Past and Future

Many of us are familiar with the patterns of dwelling on the past or worrying about the future. We replay conversations in our heads, wishing we had said something different. We ruminate over missed opportunities or think about how things could have been different. This kind of reflection, while sometimes useful for learning, can also trap us in a cycle of regret and missed chances. The past has passed.

On the flip side, we can spend an equal amount of time fixating on the future. We worry about what might go wrong, plan for every possible contingency, or fantasize about how things might be if only we get everything perfectly aligned. This preoccupation with what might come can lead to paralysis by analysis, where we're so overwhelmed by endless possibilities that we don't take any meaningful action. I don't know about you, but nothing I imagine ever works out exactly the way I envisioned it. With that understanding, it can reframe the effort and energy we expend on forecasting the future.

Embracing the Power of Now

Understanding the significance of the present moment requires a shift in perspective. When we focus on now, we're able to harness our energy and efforts towards creating something tangible. The present is where all our actions and decisions can take place and where we can build momentum towards our goals.

Consider this: Every achievement, every significant moment of our lives, is a series of choices made in the present. The greatest inventions, the deepest relationships, the most profound personal growth—these all happen in the present. They are the result of conscious decisions made in the now, not in some imagined future or long-gone past.

Practical Steps to Harness the Present

- **Mindfulness Practice.** Start incorporating mindfulness into your daily routine. This can be as simple as setting aside a few minutes each day to focus on your breathing and observe your thoughts without judgment. Mindfulness helps anchor you in the present and increases your awareness of what's happening around you and within you.
- **Set Immediate Goals.** Break down your long-term goals into actionable steps that you can take right now. Instead of getting overwhelmed by the result, focus on what you can do today to move closer to that goal. For instance, if you want to write a book, set a goal to write a page or even a paragraph each day.
- **Limit Distractions.** In our hyper-connected world, distractions are everywhere. Make a conscious effort to minimize interruptions and allocate specific times for focused work. This will help you to be more productive and present in whatever task you're engaged in.
- **Practice Gratitude.** Regularly take time to reflect on what you are grateful for in the present moment. Gratitude shifts your focus from what's lacking or what could be to appreciating what you currently have. This simple practice can enhance your overall well-being and satisfaction.
- **Act on Opportunities.** When you recognize an opportunity in the present, seize it. Don't wait for the "perfect" time or for everything to align perfectly. Acting now, even if the conditions aren't ideal, is often better than waiting indefinitely.

The Ripple Effect

Embracing the power of now doesn't just impact your immediate actions; it has a ripple effect on your entire life. When you start living more consciously in the present, you'll find that you're more attuned to opportunities, more proactive in your pursuits, and more fulfilled in your experiences. The clarity and focus gained from living in the now will spill over into other areas of your life, helping you to achieve goals, build stronger relationships, and foster a greater sense of peace and contentment.

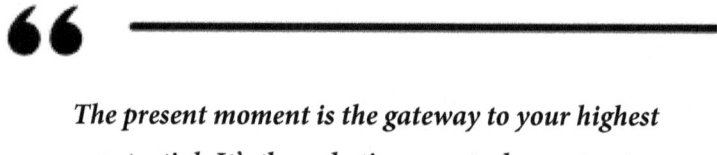

The present moment is the gateway to your highest potential. It's the only time you truly must act, to create, and to live fully.

By focusing on now, you can break free from the traps of past regrets and future worries, making the most of each moment and propelling yourself forward in ways that are meaningful and impactful. Live the power of now, and watch how it transforms your life, one present moment at a time.

Take Your Next Right Step

In what specific ways do you find yourself trapped in thoughts of the past or anxieties about the future? How might these mental habits be impacting your ability to fully engage with and appreciate the present moment?

_____

_____

_____

Think about a recent achievement or meaningful experience in your life. How was it shaped by decisions and actions you took in the present moment rather than by past regrets or future plans?

_____

_____

_____

Of the practical steps mentioned for harnessing the present (mindfulness practice, setting immediate goals, limiting distractions, practicing gratitude, and acting on opportunities), which one resonates with you the most? How could you implement this strategy in your daily life to become more present-focused?

_____

_____

_____

Overcoming Isolation

In the intricate maze of life's ups and downs, a lot of us try to get unstuck by isolating ourselves. There are common reasons why we choose a solo path over the comforting embrace of our community.

In today's hyper-connected world, the allure of digital communication from internet forums to texting and social media, can create a false sense of connection while simultaneously fostering isolation. Genuine connection, however, comes from meaningful interactions and real-life engagements, not just virtual exchanges.

The rise of the internet and social media has revolutionized how we communicate, offering unprecedented levels of connectivity at our fingertips. However, this convenience comes with a hidden cost: It's all too easy for someone who's struggling to hide from the people in their lives behind a screen. Texting and messaging platforms have become substitutes for meaningful conversations where we hear someone else's voice or share a genuine laugh together.

My friend Meg continually apologizes for her poor track record of keeping in touch with people. She, like many others, has fallen into the trap of relying only on digital communication to maintain relationships. Yet, deep down, she knows that this policy of minimal contact is not serving her well. She yearns for genuine connections and meaningful interactions but struggles to break free from the convenience and comfort of her digital cocoon. What's remarkable is that she is truly miffed when many friends have simply given up on communicating with her or when people don't immediately react when she finally wants to be in touch.

To truly combat the urge to isolate oneself, it's essential to recognize the limitations of digital communication and prioritize authentic human connection. This means making a conscious effort to engage in face-to-face interactions, picking up the phone and having a real conversation, and even scheduling regular meetups with friends and loved ones. There is no replacement for real-world connection.

While technology has undoubtedly brought us closer together in some ways, it's also important to acknowledge its shortcomings in fostering genuine connections. By recognizing the value of real-world interactions and actively seeking out opportunities for meaningful engagement, we can break free from the isolating tendencies of relying solely on technology and cultivate deeper, more fulfilling relationships with those around us.

Pride and Embarrassment Don't Help Overcome Personal Struggle

The potent interplay of pride and embarrassment forms a formidable force that influences our actions and decisions by subtly encouraging us to approach healing from personal hardships with a guarded heart. The fear of being judged or perceived as weak can cripple our willingness to open up about our challenges. This internal conflict can compel us to confront our issues in solitude. By acknowledging this dynamic, we unveil the relationship between vulnerability and the desire to maintain our private facades, facing it head-on.

After experiencing catastrophic and public losses in my life, I spent years hesitating to open up about my past to unfamiliar people. Shame and fear of judgment kept me guarded. It was only when I pushed through my apprehensions, mustering 20 seconds of courage, that I experienced deeply meaningful interactions. It is not an easy task, and fear may creep in, but sharing my struggles created a safe space where others felt comfortable sharing their own stories, fostering profound connections and mutual understanding.

Admit Your Reluctance to Burden Others

Not wishing to burden others can inadvertently create roadblocks along the path to facing challenges. As we strive for self-sufficiency, there's a tendency to resist reaching out for support. It's driven by the belief that we are sparing our loved ones from the weight of our problems. This reluctance, born from a genuine desire to shield those closest to us, becomes a paradoxical challenge in itself. The intention of being independent and resilient can subtly transform into self-imposed isolation, leaving us to contend with our concerns in solitary contemplation when we might have benefited from outside help.

This mindset stems from a deeply ingrained sense of responsibility and care for the well-being of those around us. We convince ourselves that handling our problems alone is a testament to our strength and maturity. However, this approach can lead to an overwhelming accumulation of stress and anxiety as we juggle our burdens without the relief that comes from sharing them.

Furthermore, by not seeking support, we miss out on the valuable perspectives and solutions others can offer. Our loved ones, friends, and colleagues can provide insights and advice we might not see due to our close proximity to the issue. They can also offer emotional support, which is crucial in maintaining our mental and emotional health.

Additionally, this self-imposed isolation can strain our relationships. When we don't communicate our struggles, those around us may feel disconnected or even unneeded, potentially leading to feelings of alienation on both sides. By sharing our challenges, we foster a deeper sense of trust and intimacy, allowing our relationships to grow stronger.

Recognizing that asking for help is not a sign of weakness but a demonstration of wisdom and self-awareness. It shows we understand our limits and are proactive in seeking the best possible outcomes. Embracing this perspective can lead to a healthier, more balanced approach to life's challenges, where we draw strength from our connections with others.

While the desire to avoid burdening others is noble, it is essential to balance this with the understanding that seeking support is a natural and beneficial part of human interaction. By doing so, we not only lighten our own load but also enrich our relationships, creating a supportive network that helps everyone involved navigate the complexities of life more effectively.

Overcoming Fear for Authentic Connection

Choosing to trust is an undertaking laden with uncertainty and insecurities. The challenge lies not only in acknowledging our struggles but also in anticipating how our vulnerabilities will be met by those around us. We fear judgment, misunderstanding, and even rejection. The reluctance to expose our innermost vulnerability is rooted in a hesitancy to reveal aspects of ourselves that we perceive as frail or imperfect.

Whether it's a hesitation to confide in others due to past experiences or general skepticism toward the process of seeking help, this absence of trust can impede the development of deep, meaningful connections. The fear of being too vulnerable can thwart our potential for authentic understanding and support. However, by acknowledging this struggle, we pave the way for a more profound understanding of our collective journey toward authentic connections and the transformative power of trust.

Honoring Loneliness During Difficult Times

Adversity has a unique way of sowing seeds of isolation. The weight of our struggles can create a profound sense of loneliness and prompt us to withdraw from the world. In these moments, a misleading perception takes root: the belief that we are indeed the architects of our misfortune and that that burden rests solely on our shoulders.

The universal tendency to isolate oneself during difficult times and internalize hardships may stem from a combination of factors. It might be fueled by the assumption that others won't understand our specific challenges or the fear of burdening them with our problems. The sense of being alone in our struggles constructs an emotional barrier that separates us from potential sources of empathy and support.

Like most of us, you can probably connect with the feeling of isolation during hardships, caught between the desire for understanding and the belief that we must bear our burdens in solitude. But by acknowledging this common thread, you can also unveil the profound impact of shared struggles and the potential for connection in the midst of adversity.

Don't Underestimate Others Perspective

Underestimating and appreciating the significance of external perspectives is a common inclination that deprives us of valuable insight and support. It stems from a belief that our problems are intensely personal or uniquely intricate and, therefore, beyond the help of external input. In this underestimation lies a missed opportunity to tap into the wealth of diverse viewpoints that others can offer.

The tendency to dismiss external perspectives can emerge from pride, a need for self-reliance, or a fear of vulnerability. We might convince ourselves that our challenges are too complicated for someone on the outside to understand or that our story is too unique to relate to. We think seeking advice somehow diminishes our independence. This mindset, while protective in nature, inadvertently closes the door to potentially helpful experiences and knowledge.

Realizing that the underestimation of external perspectives is a universal hurdle, a shared experience rooted in our hesitancy to expose our vulnerabilities and an assumption that our problems are different from everybody else's. By embracing the idea that external insights can illuminate our path, we open ourselves up to a broader spectrum of solutions and a deeper connection with the collective wisdom that surrounds us.

I, too, believed few could comprehend my mental health struggles. I convinced myself that my story was too unrelatable to share, holding me back from truly being authentic. It was only when I courageously shared my story, uncertain of the response, that I discovered many others were silently grappling with their own battles. This openness created unexpected bonds, allowing me to connect with others in ways I hadn't imagined possible until I embraced honesty about my challenges.

Balancing Isolation and Connection

Isolation is encouraged by the subtle influence of emotions like pride and embarrassment, which give way to the tendency to conceal one's struggles for fear of being perceived as weak. Conversely, the paradoxical challenge of balancing self-sufficiency with the human need for connection urges us to reflect on the transformative power of trust and openness.

The journey toward embracing vulnerability emphasizes the connection between the fear of judgment and the desire to maintain an ineffective facade. The noble pursuit of self-sufficiency and the genuine human need for authentic connections are at odds, but we can deepen our understanding of these complex dynamics and learn to navigate them better.

By addressing the isolating effects of adversity and dispelling the misconception that individuals alone are responsible for their misfortunes, we acknowledge the shared human experience of internalizing hardships and feeling self-imposed isolation.

I invite you to connect with the universal struggle of isolation during tough times and to embrace external perspectives as often as you can.

Take Your Next Right Step

Do you experience recurring feelings of loneliness, even when surrounded by others? Do you avoid sharing personal challenges or vulnerabilities with those closest to you?

_____

_____

_____

_____

_____

_____

Do you hesitate to seek support or share your struggles with friends, family, or colleagues, fearing judgment or burdening them unnecessarily with your problems?

_____

_____

_____

_____

Do you tend to dismiss or underestimate the value of external perspectives, believing that your problems are too personal or unique to benefit from the insight and experiences of others?

_____

_____

_____

_____

_____

Connecting Among Community

A long the path of self-discovery, I found a catalyst for transformation: the immeasurable power of community support. This revelation not only altered the trajectory of my own evolution but also became the driving force propelling me beyond the confines of stagnation.

Belonging is the cornerstone of human fulfillment. It anchors us in a sense of purpose and connection, nurturing our deepest needs for acceptance and support. When we feel truly seen and valued, we unlock our greatest potential, transforming our challenges into shared experiences and finding strength in unity. Belonging is not just a luxury—it's a fundamental human right that empowers us to thrive, grow, and contribute meaningfully to the world.

In a world increasingly defined by digital connectivity, the allure of false communities, such as those found on social media platforms, can be deceptive and overwhelming. These virtual spaces often present curated versions of reality, where individuals showcase their happiest moments and greatest achievements, creating an illusion of perfection and success. Yet, behind the polished facade lies a reality far more complex and nuanced.

As I mentioned, like many others, I have fallen prey to the trap of comparing my own journey to the highlight reels of others on social media. Scrolling through feeds filled with picturesque vacations, impressive career milestones, and seemingly perfect relationships, I couldn't help but feel inadequate in comparison. It was easy to succumb to the belief that everyone else was happier and accomplishing far more than I ever could.

However, the deeper I journeyed into self-discovery, I recognized the inherent falsehoods embedded within social media and some online communities. Behind the carefully curated posts and filtered images, there exists a multitude of struggles, insecurities, and uncertainties shared by other individuals just like me. It became increasingly clear that the true power of community lies not in the illusion of perfection but in the authenticity of shared experiences and genuine connections.

Through seeking out and nurturing genuine communities, both online and offline, I discovered a sense of belonging and support that transcended the superficiality of social media. These communities provided a space where I could openly share my triumphs and setbacks, find solace in the shared struggles of others, and receive encouragement and guidance when needed most.

In the embrace of these authentic communities, I found the strength and resilience to navigate life's challenges with greater courage and conviction. Together, we can celebrate each other's victories, lift each other up in times of need, and collectively forge a path toward growth and self-discovery.

The essence of community lies in genuine connections and shared experiences, not in the illusion of perfection. By acknowledging the limitations of superficial communities and actively seeking out spaces where authenticity prevails, we can access a source of support and inspiration that propels us forward in our journey of self-discovery and personal growth.

As I immersed myself in my chosen community, the burden that once seemed insurmountable became a shared load. The weight of my challenges, which overwhelmed me, was distributed among compassionate souls who understood the value of communal strength. Together, we shouldered these difficulties, turning what was once a solitary struggle into a collective endeavor.

Recognize the Role of Your Support System

Building a supportive community that fosters growth and resilience involves turning to those closest to us: friends and family, whether biological or chosen. Even if our personal struggles vary, these loved ones play crucial roles in creating a robust support system. Their presence and contributions are fundamental to our emotional well-being, especially in the early stages of personal transformation.

Family and friends, whether they share your background or not, can provide a solid foundation of support. Knowing you can rely on them during moments of uncertainty or distress offers significant emotional strength. They may not have faced the exact same challenges as you, but their diverse perspectives can be incredibly valuable. Their willingness to listen and offer a safe space to express your thoughts, fears, and hopes fosters an environment ripe for positive growth.

Accountability is a key component of transformation, and friends and chosen family often become vital partners in this process. They help remind you of the commitments you make to yourself and provide encouragement along the way. However, it's important to recognize and accept their limitations. No one is perfect, and expecting flawless support can strain relationships. Approach these interactions with empathy, understanding that they are doing their best within their own lives and challenges.

Accepting the imperfections of your support network means understanding that their advice and assistance may not always meet your needs perfectly. They might not always fully grasp your struggles or be able to help due to their own responsibilities and emotional limits. Understanding this reality helps set realistic expectations and fosters appreciation for their efforts, however imperfect they may be.

Forgiving any shortcomings in their support prevents resentment and strain in your relationships. Instead, cultivate gratitude for the help they provide and focus on their positive contributions to your journey. This acceptance fosters a compassionate and resilient support system where everyone is seen as allies rather than saviors.

By modeling this behavior, you encourage your friends and chosen family to extend the same grace to you, strengthening the bonds of trust and mutual support. This reciprocal process deepens your connections and makes the accountability relationship more effective and sustainable.

Friends and chosen family are not just spectators but active participants in your community. Their diverse roles and contributions create a safety net of support that enhances your journey and fosters mutual respect.

They emerge not as mere spectators but as active participants in your community. Their roles, diverse and complementary, weave a safety net of support that bolsters your endeavors.

Expanding Yourself Through Mentorship

Within my network, I discovered the impact of having accountability partners. Accountability partners can be any individual committed to the shared journey of growth. They serve as crucial guides steering you through challenges. My accountability partners' unwavering encouragement and commitment held me accountable to my aspirations, transforming mere intentions into tangible results.

Mentors offer wellsprings of wisdom that stretch beyond the boundaries of my own experiences. Their guidance, born from diverse encounters and triumphs, provided perspectives that transcended my individual focus. In this way, the journey became not only a personal quest but a collective exploration of accumulated wisdom.

The essence of community support was rooted in the vulnerability shared within its embrace. Opening up about struggles, fears, and aspirations forged connections beyond surface-level interactions. The authenticity of these relationships fostered deeper understanding, compassion, and mutual empowerment.

For me, the most transformative element was the collective energy of my supportive peer network at NAMI. As a Connection participant and then group facilitator, I witnessed many incredible stories that underscored our interconnectedness. Facing challenges together, the synergy of our shared dreams and aspirations fueled a collective sense of perseverance. In moments of doubt or weariness, the group provided inspiration and reignited my determination.

Connection through shared experience taught me that we find the strength, resilience, and inspiration needed to free us from the shackles of stagnation. Through the warmth of community, momentum is not merely gained; it becomes an unstoppable force, pushing us toward limitless horizons of growth and fulfillment.

After more than a decade of committed involvement in support communities, I've engaged with healing networks of support. Simply being present among others who understood, even when uncertain of the direction or outcome, profoundly shaped my path. My journey intertwines with individual relationships and group dynamics, all rooted in a shared pursuit of healing and personal growth.

Not every connection is meant to endure indefinitely; rather, each serves to connect us at a particular time and place.

Each step taken is a move up the staircase that brings us closer to a genuine connection with ourselves and, ultimately, with others. As we conclude this chapter, I encourage you to start thinking of your communities as a beacon illuminating the path toward a life unburdened by stagnation. Each connection can be a vital force contributing to your momentum toward a brighter, unstuck future. Embrace the tapestry of community, for within its threads lie the strength, resilience, and inspiration to forge ahead.

Take Your Next Right Step

Make a list of people you consider to be part of your village or supportive community.

Who do you know that could offer encouragement and emotional support?

_____

_____

_____

_____

Is there someone you admire who could mentor you and share their wisdom?

_____

_____

_____

_____

Do you know anyone facing similar struggles with whom you could build mutual trust and share vulnerability?

_____

_____

_____

Pick one or two people from your list to have vulnerable conversations within the next week. Share what you want to overcome and ask how they might be able to support you.

_____

_____

_____

Are key players missing from your circle? If so, make a plan to expand your network. Consider seeking mentors and peers through local groups, classes, and social media.

_____

_____

_____

Keep building a community that inspires you. Remind yourself that you don't have to get unstuck alone. We all need people to cheer us on.

Choosing Happiness

In the diverse tapestry of my own community, I stumbled upon a realization that became the linchpin of my ongoing journey: a daily commitment to choosing happiness. As I navigated the maze of personal growth, it became evident that embracing joy had an intrinsic power beyond the support of friends, family, mentors, and professionals.

It's easy to get entangled in our daily web of responsibilities, challenges, and the pursuit of success. And yet, we still have the ability to choose happiness. It isn't about ignoring difficulties or suppressing genuine emotions. Rather, it's about cultivating a mindset that seeks and recognizes happiness even in the face of adversity.

The daily practice of choosing happiness is rooted in mindfulness, or an awareness of the present moment and an intentional shift in perspective. It involves acknowledging challenges but also recognizing the beauty that exists simultaneously. This choice isn't an escape from reality. Instead, it's a conscious decision to infuse each day with positivity, gratitude, and a sense of purpose.

Communal support, as discussed in the previous chapter, is a strong foundation for this practice, but the responsibility of nurturing personal happiness rests on your shoulders. This choice is a commitment to self-love and an acknowledgment that each person contributes to the overall well-being of the community by nurturing their own happiness.

Happiness is a Choice

Choosing happiness doesn't require grand gestures. It can be as simple as finding joy in small victories, expressing gratitude for the present, or savoring the beauty of your connections within the community. It's an ongoing journey, an intentional shift in mindset that transforms the mundane into the extraordinary.

Among communities, shared joy fosters resilience. As individuals commit to their daily pursuit of happiness, the collective energy and commitment to positivity create an environment in which each person uplifts all the others.

Accountability partners, mentors, and friends contribute not only to the collective pursuit of growth but also to the shared endeavor of choosing happiness. Their support extends beyond challenges and becomes a source of joy. Celebrating successes, no matter how small, becomes an experience that strengthens communal bonds.

The significance of choosing happiness every day becomes evident in its inherent ripple effect. As individuals commit to their own well-being, the entire community benefits from the resulting contagious positive energy, inspiring others to embrace joy, gratitude, and a sense of fulfillment.

Embracing happiness must be a daily ritual, a conscious decision to nurture the soul and contribute to the vibrant energy of the community. As we navigate the complexities of life together, let us not only support each other through challenges but also celebrate the beauty of choosing everyday happiness. Within this choice lies the power to forge ahead into a future illuminated by the radiant light of shared joy.

Take Your Next Right Step

What small, daily actions can you take to cultivate a mindset of happiness, even amidst challenges?

_____

_____

_____

_____

Reflect on simple practices or rituals that bring joy and positivity into your daily routine. How can you integrate these actions to shift your perspective and focus on the positive aspects of your life?

_____

_____

_____

_____

In what ways can you actively incorporate mindfulness into your daily life to enhance your sense of happiness and gratitude?

_____

_____

_____

_____

Consider how being present and intentionally appreciating the moment can impact your overall well-being. How can mindfulness practices help you recognize and savor the beauty and joy in your everyday experiences?

_____

_____

_____

_____

How can you contribute to a positive and supportive environment within your community by choosing happiness and celebrating shared successes?

_____

_____

_____

_____

Think about the role you play in your community and how your commitment to happiness can influence others. How can celebrating small victories and expressing gratitude foster a sense of collective joy and resilience?

_____

_____

_____

_____

The Unstoppable Power of Hope

Hope is not wishful thinking; it's a compelling belief that not only helps individuals envision a brighter future but also makes it tangible and achievable. In the pursuit of the life you desire, hope becomes a guiding light, infusing every step you take with unwavering determination.

Hope is the antidote to despair and stagnation, transforming aspirations into concrete goals and dreams into reality. Nurturing hope sparks a creative vision of a future brimming with purpose, joy, and fulfillment. It empowers you to take deliberate steps toward realizing your potential and positively anticipate what lies ahead.

When we're faced with obstacles, hope provides the resilience to persevere, shifting our focus from the difficulties to the opportunities for growth and transformation on the other side.

> *Hope whispers, "This challenge is temporary, but the strength you'll gain from overcoming it will endure."*

Hope takes on a greater significance within a supportive community. Many community organizations are founded on the essence of hope, aiming to enhance lives and unite individuals with shared aspirations. In my experience with NAMI, hope flourishes through the exchange of stories among those who understand the depths of struggle. Connecting through our living experiences continues to inspire me to support others on their journey of recovery. Over my ten years as a support group facilitator, I witnessed the transformative power of just showing up as participants bravely embarked on their own path toward sustainable change.

Hope emerges as not merely wishful thinking but as a potent force that empowers us to envision and achieve a brighter future. It serves as an antidote to despair, infusing our aspirations with purpose and transforming our dreams into tangible realities. Nurturing hope fosters resilience, enabling us to persevere through challenges and embrace opportunities for growth and transformation. Within supportive communities, where shared experiences forge deep connections, hope becomes a collective energy that inspires and sustains. My journey exemplifies how hope, cultivated through empathy and shared stories, fuels personal and communal healing. It reaffirms that showing up with hope is not only the first step but a transformative path toward enduring change and fulfillment.

Take Your Next Right Step

Break down your aspirations into achievable, realistic goals. Small victories reinforce belief in the attainability of your dreams.

_____

_____

_____

_____

Remind yourself of the challenges you've overcome. Reflecting on your resilience reinforces the belief that you possess the strength to conquer future obstacles. What was the most significant challenge you overcame last week? Last month? Last year? Remember, you have survived 100% of your worst days.

_____

_____

_____

Visualize the life you desire. Create a vivid mental image of your goals and aspirations to make them feel more tangible and achievable. Describe that vision in detail. Include not only what you can see but how you feel.

_____

_____

_____

Acknowledge and celebrate each step forward. Celebrating progress reinforces the belief that positive change is always happening. What small accomplishments can you describe? How did you feel acknowledging and celebrating those?

_____

_____

_____

As we wrap up this chapter, internalize the concept that hope is not just a fleeting emotion but a steadfast companion on your journey. Embrace it, nurture it, and let it guide you forward. The life you desire is not just a distant vision but a promise fueled by the enduring flame of hope.

Conclusion
Living Unstuck

Getting unstuck and moving forward takes courage, persistence, and compassion. As we end this book, I hope that by sharing my struggles and eventual transformation, I've accurately illustrated that no matter how stuck you feel, you have the power to change.

My unraveling more than a decade ago ultimately became the greatest gift I could have received. Although it was incredibly painful and required years of committed work, it revealed a version of me that is softer, more compassionate, and kinder—to myself and others. It has allowed me to serve others from a place of true understanding and authenticity. I am inspired by the resilience of the human spirit and our capacity to begin again and again if needed. Each of us is a tapestry of our experiences, woven together to reveal the best version of ourselves.

Taking each next right step to show up for ourselves first and then for others requires steadfast courage, commitment, and consistency. This amazing journey has granted me humility from deep understanding, grace for the known and unknown, and the capacity to explore more deeply even when I struggle to find light. Today, I am proud to serve others who are striving toward their best selves in the same way I showed up to serve myself.

In my roles as founder and president of the for-profit organization Connection Project, president and CEO of the non-profit National Alliance of Mental Illness for Arapahoe and Douglas Counties, host of the *Get*

Unstuck. Move Forward with Your Life radio show and creator of the Nobody's Perfect Community (an online platform of clinician-approved mental health resources for youth, parents, caregivers, providers, and educators), I am dedicated to walking alongside other champions who seek their best selves.

Wherever you are in your life today, you can make your way to your heart's desire. By using the tools you've learned in this book, you have the capacity to:

- Shift your mindset.
- Reframe your perception of past hurts.
- Quiet your inner critic.
- Take ownership of your path.
- Surround yourself with positive support.
- Consistently take the next right step.

True progress is slow and nonlinear. You will stumble along the way. But now, you can draw on the skills you have learned and your inner wisdom and strength to correct your course as needed. Use setbacks as fuel to keep moving ahead, and do not diminish your efforts by worrying about having to start small; tiny steps will reveal something beautiful when you take many of them.

Your past pain can equip you to lift others up. The messiness you have overcome can become an inspirational message. Everything you have conquered has provided you with the empathy, passion, and wisdom you need to find your purpose.

One day, you will look back and feel grateful for every obstacle you encountered, knowing that each one helped shape you into the person you always wanted to become. Sharing this truth will inspire fellow travelers to keep going, too.

Stay focused on the horizon ahead while living in alignment with your current values. Keep showing up for yourself with compassion and love; you are worth it.

> *You are not defined by your past or limited by conditions, nor are you broken beyond hope. You are resilient and ready.*

Take a deep breath; your best life is still ahead. Now, boldly take the next right step forward and claim it.

Onward and upward!

And remember, you don't have to embark on this journey alone. I invite you to stay connected with me through my radio show, *Get Unstuck. Move Forward with Your Life* and my socials @getunstuckradio on Facebook, Instagram, LinkedIn, TikTok, Twitter, and YouTube.

Tune in for inspiration, guidance, and support as you boldly work to get unstuck. Together, we can empower each other to embrace change and the fulfilling lives we deserve.

THANK YOU FOR READING MY BOOK!

Thank you for reading my book!

Download Your Free Gifts
My Honesty Report Card and the Plutchik Emotion Wheel

Scan the QR Codes:

Your Feedback Matters! Thank you for reading my book. Your thoughts are invaluable in helping me improve future editions. I would be grateful if you could share your honest review on Amazon.com.

www.ingramcontent.com/pod-product-compliance
Lightning Source LLC
Chambersburg PA
CBHW070120100426
42744CB00010B/1882